My Calling

Merrill Phillips

Order this book online at www.trafford.com
or email orders@trafford.com

Most Trafford titles are also available at major online book retailers.

Printed in the United States of America.

ISBN: 978-1-4669-3251-7 (sc)
ISBN: 978-1-4669-3250-0 (e)

Trafford rev. 06/27/2012

www.trafford.com
North America & international
toll-free: 1 888 232 4444 (USA & Canada)
phone: 250 383 6864 ♦ fax: 812 355 4082

TOUCHED BY GOD'S OMNIPOTENT HAND

The following is an account of my personal experiences with God and how He has blessed me through His Son, Jesus Christ and the Holy Spirit. I feel very blessed to have been guided and helped through this life by the love of our Lord and Savior, Jesus Christ. Perhaps someday my experiences will give someone the inspiration that they need in seeking the Lord's help in their own life.

Some may say that my experiences were nothing but the figment of my imagination. They have the right to believe any way that they wish, but when such experiences happen, they are real. Jesus Christ is real and He heals and guides people just as He did when He lived among us.

God does groom those whom He chooses to serve Him. While going through adverse situations one cannot see anything but the problems that confront them, but when looking back on their lives they can see how God had worked in their life to prepare them for service to Him.

The following is an account of what God allowed me to go through to change my heart and prepare me to write what he wanted to convey to others. It has been the most humbling experience of my life. When going through those experiences I had no idea of what was going on, for God does not say, "I want you to serve me, this is what I want you to do to get ready." Some of the experiences were very trying and taxing, both physically and spiritually. Only by looking back on them could I tell that they were for my spiritual growth.

I am not telling these experiences to brag about how God worked in my life, but to show that no one is prepared to work on God's behalf without going through a period of preparation. Sometimes this period is relatively short and sometimes it takes years, which it was in my case. I was in my mid-twenties when I had my first experience and in my sixties when God told me, "Take pen and paper and write." It matters not the length of time, what does matter is if one answers their calling or refuses to for whatever reason. At first, I made all kinds of excuses not to write, from not being qualified for such an endeavor to I was a bad speller, but eventually I chose to answer my calling and have never regretted that decision. We may not be qualified for our calling but God will supply whatever we need if we but allow Him.

God is without a doubt the greatest teacher and friend anyone could ever have. I have and will continue to praise him for what he has done on my behalf and how He has changed me through trials and tribulations. I serve God with a humble heart and assign to Him all of the glory and honor that may or may not be bestowed upon me. Without His intervention in my life, today I would be a lost soul without hope of redemption or salvation. Glory be to God now and forevermore.

I write this in humility to let others know that when they are going through hard times that they are meant for their spiritual growth, thus bringing them closer to their creator, God.

Many fail in the process of changing their lives and live lives unfit for the kingdom of God as witnessed by daily news reports from around the world. The few who do answer their calling do it without fanfare and not for self-satisfaction, but do it for the advancement of God's kingdom here on earth and hope for a better future for all.

No greater honor can be bestowed upon anyone than to serve God. This brings the stories as told in the Bible alive and as relevant today as when they were first recorded for our benefit in our time and place in the history of humankind.

Thank God for His loving and caring ways in which He holds all, regardless of their nationality or color of skin. God looks on the internal, not the external and calls all according to His purpose.

1   In 1948 the year before my first wife and I were married, we built a new house and it was not finished until after we were married. Our bedroom was on the second floor, we had studs for walls and the ceiling was the bear roof. One night while we slept I experienced my spirit leaving my body and ascending up through the roof. As I ascended up into the sky I remember looking down and seeing myself sleeping in bed beside my wife. The night was clear, the stars shone bright and I could see the most of the town in which we lived.

I do not know just how high I went, but there was no sensation of being cold or that there might be something wrong. It was all very peaceful. For whatever reason I suddenly became aware that I was rising higher and higher, and then I became aware that I was descending, I went back down through the roof and my spirit reentered my body. Through the whole experience, I felt no sensation of fear or of pending harm. If this in fact was a dying experience, I know that dying is not something to be feared.

2   One Wednesday night while attending Bible study at our church we were all seating in a circle discussing the Bible and its relationship to man. There was a cricket in the room and it was making itself know by its loud chirping. Some of the women tried to find the cricket so that they could kill it, thus preventing it from making any kind of a mess. I went to the general area where it was, kneeling down I put my hand on the floor with my palm up. The women moved different objects in their search for the cricket and the cricket came out of its hiding place, hopped over to me, hopped up into my hand, and stopped. I closed my hand, took the cricket outside, and let it loose in the grass.

3   While attending the same church I served as an usher, before every service the ushers conducted a devotional and each week a different usher conducted the meeting. On a Saturday, I came down with symptoms of the flue and by Sunday morning, I did not feel like going to church, but I went anyway. During the usher's devotional,

while one of the ushers was praying I began to feel better, the fever left me and by the time, church services were over I was completely well and to this day in 2011, I have never had the flue since. I have been exposed to the flue many, many times over the years and have never come down with it or any symptoms. This healing took place in 1958.

4 The following year I had a very unpleasant encounter with Satan. One day while walking up the stairs to the second floor to tell my wife that I was going with my next-door neighbor (Henry) to see a ship that had grounded in a near-by town. As I climbed the stairs a voice spoke to me and told me to kill, it never said who or how, but to just kill. With the command to kill came an urge to do what Satan had just told me to do. It was almost overwhelming and could not be put aside. The urge to kill kept getting stronger and it took all of the strength that I could muster to keep from killing someone, anyone. It almost overwhelmed me, but I stood fast in the love of God and kept denying Satan. I knew deep within my heart that it was wrong and I kept repeating the truths of God that I knew at the time and in this way, I kept from doing what that voice had told me to do. I knew that it was from Satan and knew that God was more powerful than Satan was and if I could hold fast to the truths of God, then Satan could not have his way with me. This was without a doubt the greatest fight that I would ever be in, a fight for my very soul.

After some weeks, the urge to kill began to subside, it was a constant battle to control and it took over a year before it was to the point that it was not a daily urge. It did however raise its ugly head when least expected, by then I knew that I could control that urge through God and did not hesitate to call upon God for help whenever it tried to raise its ugly head. I did not intend to obey that evil voice, but it certainly was not an easy task to stand up and deny it. I never told my wife or anyone about that experience.

Even today, when I think about that encounter with Satan it gives me chills to think of what would have happened if I had given in to Satan. At the same time, I found out firsthand just how powerful the word of God really is and that He loved me enough to help me through such an experience and I will always be indebted to God for His help.

After going through such an experience, I have an understanding of why some people kill for no apparent reason, but I also know that there is a way out of such a dilemma, and that is through our loving God in heaven.

5   After my first wife divorced me in 1962 to seek her fortune elsewhere she sent our youngest daughter to a private school. Just before Christmas one year, my daughter called me and wanted me to meet her and her mother at the train station just outside of Boston so that she could do some Christmas shopping. I reluctantly agreed to meet them even though I had no desire to do so, just

because her mother would be there, I had no desire to see her mother, and the less I had to do with her the better. She had had a son by her new husband and this in itself created a situation that I wanted nothing to do with. I went for the sole reason that my daughter had asked me.

After arriving at the train station, I met my x-wife and we were polite to one another and made small talk without talking about the past. She had brought her young son (about four months old) with her. During our conversation, I went over and looked at the baby as he lay in his carrier. He was a handsome child and as I was looking at him, he just smiled at me and through his smile, he expressed nothing but love. At that very moment, all of the hate, bitterness and animosity that I had held since our breakup just melted away. I could feel a great weight being lifted from my shoulders. At last, I was free from all of the hostility and the feeling of wanting revenge and of hurting her for what she had done to me. We did go Christmas shopping and I enjoyed it. I had received the greatest Christmas gift of all. God had freed me from a situation that could have made me bitter for the rest of my life.

Today my first wife and my present wife and I are best of friends. She is often a guest in our home. We socialize and in general enjoy one another's company. I tell this to show that through God all things are possible and that when we let go and allow God to work His wonders there is no need for hate, revenge or the worst of circumstances to ruin our lives. God meters out justice in His time and in His way. Out of chaos comes victory if we allow God to work in our lives.

6 A couple of years later I re-married and before the marriage the Lord spoke to me and told me, "There will be no children by this marriage." During this eight-year marriage, there were no children. This marriage too ended up in divorce, mostly because I was not fully over my feelings for my first wife. Though I seldom saw her, I still had feelings for her that were never satisfied.

7 before my second divorce I started a relationship with another woman and became very fond of her and would have married her, but she had recently been divorced and was not sure of what she wanted to do. Then one day as we were on our way to lunch, the Lord spoke to me and said, "This relationship will not work." Within two weeks, we broke up and went our separate ways.

8 One weekend I visited my parents, I was single at the time and was drinking more than I should have been. I had had quite a bit to drink and my older brother came over and told me that if I wanted to go out drinking that he would go with me. He knew all of my matrimonial problems and was trying to console me. For whatever reason I did not feel like going out, so we just sat around and talked for a while and during that conversation, I expressed the desire to live a more Christ-like life, but did not know how. I realized years later that that moment was my turning point in my relationship with Jesus Christ.

9   I was in the plumbing and heating business at the time and one of the supply houses where I bought most of my plumbing and heating supplies from offered an air conditioning course and it was to be held in Nashville Tenn. I decided to take the course and while in Nashville, I called my x-sister in-law who lived in Jackson Ms. and she invited me down for the following weekend. I declined her invitation, but later in the week I changed my mind, called her back, and told her I would be down to see her and her husband that weekend. Her husband met me at the airport and informed me that his wife had set me up with a blind date for the weekend. My sister in-law informed me that she and her husband had a previous engagement for that Saturday night, but my date would pick me up and later on they would join us for dinner. The next afternoon about six o'clock this car drove in the driveway and a woman knocked at the door. When I opened the door, she introduced herself as Nell Brown and that she was my blind date for the evening. By the time my sister in-law and her husband joined us for dinner Nell and I had discussed our backgrounds and I came to the conclusion that Nell was going to be my next wife. When my sister in-law asked me what I thought of Nell, I replied, "If you come to visit me do not be surprised if Nell answered the door." We found out that we both had the same birthday date, though not the same year. Six months later, we were married on our birthday and at this writing, we have been married for thirty-five years. We celebrate our birthdays and anniversary on the same date.

Before Nell and I met, we both had declared that we were through with marriage, mostly because we both had gone through two marriages that did not work and had consoled ourselves to a life without a spouse. I firmly believe that when we gave up on marriage God stepped into the picture and brought us together. At this writing we have been married for thirty-five years and have enjoyed and have no regrets making the decision to try marriage again.

10 I had an alcohol problem for quite a few years and at the time Nell and I lived in New Hampshire where I ran my Plumbing and Heating business. I really did not like the taste of alcohol, but after the first drink, the taste did not make much difference. Every night before going to sleep, I repeated the Lord's Prayer and asked God to remove alcohol from my life. The alcohol and blood pressure medication that I was taking did not go well together and it was affecting my kidneys to the point where they were hurting most of the time except when I was drinking. The alcohol numbed the pain and this gave me an excuse to keep on drinking. Even so the more I drank the worse the situation was getting and I knew within myself that if I did not give up alcohol it would not be too long before my kidneys failed.

We had the tradition of having a New Year's party with a big bonfire and as many as sixty or so people would attend. There was no shortage of alcohol. In 1980, we had our last party. Of course, I had too much to drink and went to bed around one to two o'clock in the morning. As usual, I repeated the Lord's Prayer when I went to bed and sometime during the night, I had a spiritual experience that changed my life and from that moment on, I have never taken a drink of alcohol.

During that night, I had a vision in which I witnessed a bright "Light" about the size of a basketball way off in the distance. There was nothing but complete darkness and slowly this "Light" moved ever closer and as it did it grew in size and brilliance until finally I was completely engulfed in the "Light". The "Light" was so bright that no human eyes could look upon the "Light" without going blind. Even as bright as the "Light" was it cast no shadows, nor was it in any way threatening.

My first instinct was one of fear and I called out to the "Light", "Go away, leave me alone." In response, the "Light" began to recede. At that very moment, I knew what the "Light" was and why it was there. I knew the "Light" was the "Light" of Jesus Christ. I cannot explain how I knew, I just knew. As the "Light" started to move away, I called out to the "Light", "Come back, please come back." In response, the "Light" once again began to move towards me and grow brighter again, as much as to say, "Yes, it is I." The "Light" stayed for a period of time and then receded, as it receded it grew smaller in size but retained its brilliance until it vanished from my sight. How long this vision lasted, I have no idea.

When I awoke the next day, I had lost all desire for alcohol and in a week, my kidneys returned to normal and have been so ever since. This was a life changing experience and I thank God for it.

11 A couple of years after this experience the Lord told me, "You will not have enough money to retire on." Now that I am in my retirement years, I do not have enough money to completely retire. I often do odd jobs to make ends meet. I have come to the realization that in God telling me this that He will supply me and my wife with everything that we will need, for God's hand is never empty for those who love Him. I have also come to realize that retirement is not the ultimate, doing the will of God is.

12 In nineteen and eighty three Nell and I were on our way to live in Arizona. My youngest daughter (Pauline) and her husband lived in St. Louis, Mo. On our way, we stopped to see them. Pauline informed us that she was going to have a baby and asked if we would stay at least until the baby was born. Two and a half years later, we left St. Louis and moved to Arizona.

While we lived in St. Louis, my grandmother Phillips visited me on three different occasions. The unusual thing about it was that my grandmother died in the fall of 1946.

The first time she visited me was at night while I slept. I was awakened by the feeling that someone was standing next to me while I slept. I sat straight up in bed, wide-awake. I watched as a translucent figure walked from my side, around the foot of the bed, through the open bedroom door and disappeared down the hallway.

A few days later, she awoke me in the same manner. This time she walked to the foot of the bed, through the bureau and the wall and disappeared from view.

The third time she awoke me in the same manner. This time she walked over to the bathroom door (The master bathroom was off the bedroom) and then she turned towards me to where I could see her face and this is when I realized that the translucent figure was my grandmother. She was wearing a full length white like robe and she was wearing her favorite hat that she used to wear whenever she went somewhere special. The hat was from the 1930 era. It had artificial fruit on it, apple, banana and a clump of purple grapes. She then turned and walked into the bathroom and disappeared from view.

My grandmother died from cancer and at the time of her death, she weighted around seventy pounds or so. Her normal weight was between one hundred and thirty to one hundred and forty pounds. When she visited me, she was as she was before she had cancer, normal in all respects. She never spoke to me or made any jesters as to why she had come to see me. I concluded that she wanted to show me that she was all right. This experience alone proved to me that there is life beyond the grave. This experience also raised many questions. How did she know where I lived, for she herself had never been to St. Louis when she was alive? To find me in such a large city still boggles my mind. What was her purpose for visiting me? Perhaps she wanted to convey to me that she was now with our Lord and Savior, Jesus Christ. I will one day find the answers when I pass from this life to eternal life, till then I will be satisfied in knowing that she isn't really dead, just living in a different dimension than we here on earth.

13 While living in St. Louis my wife and I went on a trip to Mississippi and on the way home; we stopped at a restaurant for lunch. After parking the car and before we got out of the car, a stranger approached us and he asked for a quarter with which to buy a cup of coffee. He was dressed in shabby clothes and he said that he worked on the river and had many times been through St. Louis on riverboats. Because of the time of year, he had not worked for quite some time due to the ice that blocked the river in some places. We gave him a couple of dollars and he walked away. After he left, we both felt as though we should have given him more money, we got out of the car and looked around for him and he was gone. He did not have time enough to get very far and yet he was nowhere to be found. We looked in the restaurant, up and down the street and could not find him. He just disappeared. Angel or just a down and out river man?

14 While living in Sun City, Arizona we went to Laughlin Nevada to do some gambling. While there, we stayed in one of the local motels. In

the afternoon, we went to our room to rest, as I walked through the door of our room a voice spoke to me and said, "Take pen and paper and write." I stood there in amazement and said to myself, "Write? I can't write, I know nothing about writing. I hardly passed English when I was in high school, let alone write." About a year later, I started writing and have been writing ever since.

15 After leaving Arizona we moved to Farina, Illinois where I managed an apple orchard for three years. During pruning season, I would save the limbs and trees that had to be removed and cut them up for firewood to burn during the winter months. One day as I was storing some of this wood in the woodshed a voice spoke to me and said, "You will not be here to burn any of this wood." Sure enough a couple of months later the orchard owner called me on the phone and informed me that he was closing the orchard the first of the year and that my job would be terminated at that time.

16 After leaving Farina we moved to Canton, Ms. where I worked as a janitor for a Baptist Church. Here I met one of my co-workers and we had many discussions about Jesus Christ and our relationship with Him. It was a time of spiritual growth. A friend had asked me for a loan of money and I was torn as to whether to make the loan or not. One day while working in the sanctuary I sat down in one of the pews, took the Bible, and opened it in search of an answer. The Bible opened to Acts 20:25. I have shown

you all things, how that so laboring ye ought to support the weak, and to remember the words of the Lord Jesus, how he said, It is more blessed to give than receive. This settled the issue; I made the loam with a new perception that we are to help our neighbor if we have it within our power to do so.

17 While living in Canton I had a woodworking shop and made crafts and sold them at different flea markets. One of those flea markets was in St. Louis Mo . . . My daughter still lived there and she would go to the flea market with me. On one trip, the engine in my van started to leak oil on the main bearing and as a result, I had to stop every hundred mile and put in more oil. I started to pray about the situation and after a couple of more stops to put oil in the engine I saw a finger wrap around the main bearing of the engine and much to my surprise and amazement the engine quite leaking oil. It never did leak oil again. It may seem strange but God will answer prayers in ways that we cannot comprehend.

18 After leaving Canton Ms. we moved to Byhalia, Ms. that is in the northern part of the state, just a short distance from Memphis Tn . . . I had a job with a heavy construction company. One morning my alarm did not go off and I awoke thirty minutes later than normal. I hurried and while on the way to work a police car with its lights on had the road blocked. He told me that I could not go through because there had been an accident in an intersection that I passed through every morning. It turns out that if I had been

on time that morning I would have been in that intersection at the same time as the accident. Without touching the alarm clock the next day and after that, my alarm went off when it should.

19 I started to have a pain in my right side and each day it seemed to get worse. While driving the company truck on my rounds to different supply houses to pick up parts for the heavy equipment I was listening to a Christian radio station and the announcer was asking for prayer for a couple who was having matrimonial problems. Having been through divorce, I felt a kinship to their problem and while I prayed on their behalf, I felt a twinge in my right side and the hurting stopped. Over the next few days my pain and problem was gone completely.

20 During sleeping hours one night I found myself in a protective compartment traveling through the sky at such speed that the stars were as blurred streaks of light. How far I had gone or how long I have no idea. I believe that God was showing me that when we leave this earth that we are protected on our way to heaven. I have no other explanation.

21 In 2010, God again spoke to me and said, "It is time to slow down." Shortly after that, my writing slowed down and the desire to quit full time work became stronger and stronger. At eighty four and a half, I gave up my full time job and now spend my days compiling my writings and doing a little part time work.

22 Ever since my auto accident on Sept 9, 2009 I have had problem with my neck. It snaps and cracks at times and can be very uncomfortable. One day it was especially uncomfortable and unexpectedly I told the Holy Spirit that I needed his help with it and almost instantly, the pain and uncomfortableness left. Since then my neck has been much better and free from pain.

To this date, I have written close to two thousand different articles. The majority of them are about spirituality, children stories, and stories of the sea. They have all been inspired by the Holy Spirit and for the most part were written during the night hours. Never once have I awoken in the morning and felt tired from the lack of sleep because of writing. I have been blessed many times over for answering God's call for me to write. Without Him and his guidance, this would not have been possible. Many of them have been put on the internet and have had one request from India to translate them into their local language. Have received different comments from many different countries. I can only thank God for making this possible.

ALL FOR THE GLORY OF GOD

If I have but touched one heart through my writings, I will rejoice and give praise unto the Lord. I cannot change the way one thinks or acts, I can only encourage them to improve their lives by accepting Jesus Christ as their Lord and Savior.

I hope that some of the seed I cast will fall on fertile ground. Others may water that seed and yet others may cultivate and remove the weeds that will grow along with the newly sprouted seeds until the newly gained spiritual life is strong enough to help promote the kingdom of God here on earth.

It is imperative that all who have a desire to spend eternity in the presence of God that they take control of their lives and seek a personal relationship with the one who created this wonderful world and devote their time becoming a child of God, rather than seeking worldly riches that satisfy for the moment and in the end leave one high and dry with nothing but a false sense of security.

It can be a long hard road to follow to accomplish what God has for someone to do, but through perseverance they will one day come to realize that the trials of life they may have suffered was to prepare them for whatever God wanted them to do for Him. Following the calling of God can and will be the greatest experience that anyone could ever have in this life. Not that they will become rich and famous, for God offers not riches and notoriety, just the inner feeling that one is doing what the creator of all has called them to do. God does and will complete one's life and make life worth living. God prepares different people in different ways, but the results will be the same.

Many struggle with the idea that God has called them to serve Him. I was that way when God called me to "take pen and paper and write." I knew nothing about writing or how to go about putting thoughts on paper. Over time after making excuses to myself for feeling inadequate, I wrote a short note thanking the congregation of the church that my wife and I were attending at the time for their generosity that they had shown on our behalf. This was the beginning of my writing career. Writing for God has enhanced my knowledge of God and His plan for my life. I would have never chosen writing for me because English and spelling were my worst subjects in school and besides who was I to be favored in such a manner?

Do not be shy about sharing with others what God has done in your life. Become as a farmer and cast your seeds before men and God will honor you for your efforts. Doing the will of God will be laying up of treasures in heaven and receiving your rewards in the life that lies beyond the grave. One of God's promises is that He will supply our every need in this life; therefore, no one has a legitimate excuse for not serving God. As difficult, as it may be to comply with ones calling it will be the highlight of one's life.

God is in the business of calling people to serve Him here on earth. However God leaves it up to each individual as to whether they want to serve Him or not. God gave us free will and will honor our decisions about our own lives, but wouldn't it be better to err on the side of God rather than to have to face God on judgment day and explain why we did not follow our calling? As we find in the scriptures, Jesus said, "If you deny me before men I will deny thee before my Father".

It is God's will that we honor Him here on earth and become as little children sitting before the throne of God seeking His love and protection. Praise God and honor Him by being obedient children here on earth.

A CROSS ON A FAR AWAY HILL

With the light from above, I go there every night in
hopes of seeing my Lord on high.

To receive from him the blessings that will carry
me through the hard days that lie ahead.

It gives me the assurance that I am not alone in
a world that tries to hold me at bay.

When I see that light I know that He loves me and
I need not worry what this world can do to me.

If I keep my eyes on that cross, one day I will be able
to enjoy the freedom that it represents for those
who follow Him.

A greater joy no man can have than the sight of that
cross on that far away hill.

It gives me hope when all hope is gone of my
surviving the ills of this world.

Its light burns deep within my soul and I can
feel its warmth on days when things
go wrong.

A greater sight my eyes will never behold than
a cross on that hill far away.

A GUIDE TO A MORE ABUNDANT LIFE

Use the Bible as a standard by which you live your life, let not the deceivers of this world turn your head, for in doing so you deny God and His plan for your life.

Man will boast of his deeds and proclaim them a guide for all to follow, when in fact they lead to the gates of hell and beyond.

The truths found in the Bible can turn the most ardent fool into a follower of Jesus Christ and an asset to his friends and family and a promoter of the gospel to all they meet.

Left unchallenged the word of man can bring a nation to the edge of destruction, whereas the word of God can bring a nation to its fullest potential.

The pages of the Bible are full of accounts that have brought the most violent men to their knees, becoming a blessing to the advancement of God's kingdom here on earth.

Where else but the Bible can one turn and find peace of mind, soul, and body? The bible is surly a guide by which one should live their life, it proclaims truth, truth that can and will set man free from the bondage of sin.

Satan may attack from all sides, but Biblical truth can dull the spears of lies that Satan uses in his battle against God, the Bible and what it stands for. The content of the Bible can keep Satan's spears of lies from penetrating the armor of truth.

To adhere to anything but the truths of the Holy Scriptures or other inspired writings would be the wrong path to follow, for all other documents are of Satan, meant to draw people away from the basic truths of scripture, leading them to eternal death.

Jesus Christ, the Son of God, is the centerpiece of the scriptures, our hope, our salvation, the doorway to eternal life, for no one comes to the Father except through the Son of God, Jesus Christ. He and He alone holds the key to eternal life and He will give it to all who submit to his will.

The "Love" of Jesus Christ can change the heart and brighten the soul so that we can shine as a lighthouse in the midst of the storms of life, a "Love and Light" that cannot be extinguished no matter how hard Satan might try.

The scriptures lead to a new beginning, a new life, one free from the bondage of sin and instills in us a desire to serve God rather than man. We become free to express ourselves as the Bible encourages us to do, free to live a life more pleasing to God.

All of these changes are laid out in the pages of the Bible, adhere to them and become the person that God intends for you to be, turn from the ways of the world, become a child of God and receive the blessings that come with change, be a friend to your fellowman rather than a curse.

Our redemption draws neigh, the time fast approaches when the tares shall be separated from the wheat and cast into the fires of hell, there will wailing and gnashing of teeth.

The winds of time are soon to silenced by the return of our Lord and Savior, Jesus Christ, then all accounts will be settled and each and everyone will be assigned their chosen place in the pages of the history of mankind, now is the time to choose from the only two choices there are, heaven or hell.

Let not your epitaph read, "I chose death (sinful ways) over life, for it fulfilled my every desire to live life my way.", but rather strive to do the will of the one who created you and have your epitaph read, "Well done good and faithful servant, come, enjoy the fruits of your labor, rest in My peace and love forever and ever."

A NEW LIFE

When I step through the door of death what a wonderful sight I will see, the greatest sight that there will ever be.

Friends and relatives will greet me by the score, Jesus will grasp me by the hand and welcome me to my new home.

I will hear Him say, "Welcome my child, we all have been waiting for you. Come, join us and we will celebrate your return.

The grass, flowers, and the trees will dazzle my eyes with their beauty, they will extend to the distant sea.

It is a place where the sheep will graze with the lion, the children shall play with the serpent and no harm shall befall them.

My eyes shall behold the glory of God, my feet shall walk on the streets of gold.

I shall quench my thirst with the waters that flows from the throne of God, O how sweet.

My feet will be weary no more as I travel form place to place, drinking in the beauty that will lie before me.

There will be no more darkness where sin can hide, no more shadows to follow me as I go about fulfill the will of God.

No more sunrises or sunsets, for the "Light" of God shall illuminate this place of paradise.

Paradise is reserved for those who forsook the ways of the flesh and walked the path that is straight and narrow.

No more worldly cares to burden me down, no more toil or pain, just the love of God to comfort my soul.

A PATHWAY FROM HEAVEN TO EARTH

O clouds where art thou, come quickly and bring
our lord back to stay.

We stand gazing into the heavens above, wide eyed
in anticipation of His return.

At night we dream of the day when He will walk
with us and watch over His sheepfold.

The great Shepherd He was and the great Shepherd
He will always be.

He will lead His sheep to green pastures and give
them water from the river of life.

Where are you who will provide him with a path
from heaven to earth? Tarry not O cloud.

Your sheep await Your return O Lord, they wait
day and night, anxious to gaze upon Your
countenance and praise Your
Holy name.

We await the day when the clouds of heaven will
part and behold the Lord Jesus will appear
in all of His glory.

He will gather unto Himself the sheep of His flock
and cast the goats into the lake of fire,
there will be weeping and gnashing
of teeth.

For now all we can do is wait and prepare ourselves for that which is to come.

Let it be as He said, a time known only by His Father, above.

A SPECIAL PLACE

There is a place through the woods and around the
next bend that belongs to you and me.

A place where time meets time, it had no beginning,
it has no end.

A place where the presence meets the past, and the
future is forever now.

A place where the skies are always blue, the breezes
are fresh and fair.

A place where there are only friends, it was created
for those who love and are loved in return.

A place where the angels of heaven stand at the gates
and only allow the pure in heart to enter therein.

A place where shrubs and flowers grace the land, the
animals are gentle and roam free.

A place where there is no more tears nor pain, no more
sickness or death, only peace and love that
heretofore we never knew.

A place where power, glory and honor belongs to God, for
He resides in this special place through the
woods and around the next bend.

A SYNOPSIS OF LIFE

Fifty, sixty, seventy years or more seems like a long time, but in the scheme of things, it is but the wink of an eye. To look back and remember the things of childhood when life was carefree brings back memories of playing for hours and wishing that you would grow up fast so that you could do the same things that the older children were doing.

Then came the day when you looked at the opposite sex as more than someone to play and fight with. You began to develop and go through those self-conscious stages, stumbling all over yourself when that certain person said, "Hi, how are you today." You seek for words but nothing comes but an awkward, "OK or just fine." You get all red faced and wish that you could just disappear.

Then the school years pass so quickly, what fun you had playing team sports or just watching them, trying to be as good as you thought you could be. During this time true love hits and no one else will do, for a while at least, until the next heartthrob came along. Not that you were fickle minded, but what the hay, why stay with just one when there are so many good lookers around.

Then comes the day when the right Mr. or Miss Right comes along. One who captured your heart from the first time you looked at them. Awkwardly at first, then as time passes you realize that this is the person that you want to spend the rest of your life with. After taking your new found love home with you to meet your family you agree to get married and settle down. Then comes the day when you no longer are just playing house like you did as a child, you are now playing house for real with all of its heartaches and joys.

When your first child is born, you think that no one in the world has ever had a child any finer than yours, both mom and dad are as proud as can be. Then your child begins their journey through life. This in turn brings back memories of your own childhood that you thought had been put to rest a long time ago. You follow their growth with the same interest that your folks had following yours. You both give your child the love and attention that you once had received. Their school years become yours all over again. Then before you realize it, it is their time to leave home and the cycle starts all over again. Through it all, you stand by your child Just as your folks had stood by you.

One-day father time taps you on your shoulder and says, "Happy Birthday" you have reached your fiftieth, sixtieth, or seventieth birthday. Everyone wishes you a happy birthday and wish you many more joyous years ahead. However, in your heart you know that your time here on earth will soon come to an end and that soon you will join your parents in the life that comes after death. These thoughts sadden you for a while, then you reconcile yourself to the fact that this is the way things have to be and you smile with the contentment of having had a good and productive life and that it will soon be your time to leave this life behind.

This is the way life has been since the beginning of mankind. God created us all and gave unto all their own number of years here on earth. We can neither add to that amount of years nor take away from it. Live life to glorify God and one day you will come to understand the whys and wherefores of our earthly existence.

A WALK
THROUGH LIFE

Just think there is a completely different world out there, one that we know very little about. The only way that we can be a part of this, new world is to pass from the life that we now are experiencing. God knew us before we entered into this life; of this, we have no recollection. Through God's wisdom, He has given us a record of man through the pages of the Bible, a record that demonstrates God's love for His created beings and a means by which man can be saved from the sins of the world.

We walk this life shrouded in the clouds of sin and blinded by the lusts of the flesh. We stumble and sometimes fall to the temptations of Satan, forever forbidden to enter the kingdom of God without repenting of our sins through Jesus Christ. When we hit rock bottom with no other place to turn, some will turn to God for help. Their excuses being, "Even though I do not believe in God, what do I have to lose? I have tried everything else; perhaps there is something to this God that others are talking about." At this point the clouds of sin that we have been walking through begins to dissipate and a beam of light shines through and for the first time in our life we feel the warmth and love that God has for all seek Him. This can make dramatic changes in our life and lifestyle and if we revert to our old lifestyle, we now have a place to go for help in our struggle with the temptations of sin.

If we allow ourselves to succumb to the temptations of Satan, it can indeed be very difficult to escape from his influence in our lives. While under the influence of Satan, we lose sight of what is right and wrong and go about life in complete disregard for our spiritual life. The more we indulge in gaining personal wealth, power, prestigious positions in our business life or whatever we think will make us happy, the more we come under the influence of Satan's deceitful ways and the less we pay attention to what the Bible admonishes us to do. Many will die in their sins and never come to the realization that they face eternity separated from God. This is Satan's goal, to blind people to the truths of God, Satan cares nothing about us or who we are except to destroy our faith and trust in God.

Deep inside we know when we do right or wrong, it is when we allow the wrongs in life to control our lives that we become in danger of the damnation. It is then time to come before the throne of Jesus Christ and confess our sins, asking for forgiveness of our sins and in turn, Jesus Christ will forgive us our sins and restore us to our rightful place in His sheepfold.

Sin, like darkness cannot survive where the "Light" of God shines. The "Light" of God casts no shadows where sin can hide. The sun leaves one-half of this world in darkness, but God's "Light" bathes the whole world in "Light" and there is no darkness found anywhere. All who come to the "Light" will be cleansed from all unrighteousness and live a more Christ-like life, seeking and doing the will of God in their lives.

Our walk through life is what we make it, we may be influenced by the actions of others, but it is our decision as to allow that influence to affect our lives or not. It is easier to blame others for our own shortcomings, than it is to admit that we are wrong and need to change our ways. Blaming others is just another way of getting out of our responsibility to admit our wrongs and making the necessary changes. We are admonished to forgive those who trespass against us and love them as God loves us, thus receiving forgiveness of our own trespasses against others. Those who reject change in their lives will one day face their day of judgment and will be judged by the same standards that they judged others, and then will justice be served.

Walk in the paths of righteousness by doing the will of God in your life and you will dwell in the house of the Lord forever, reject Him and face the fires of hell. Let not the trials of this life weigh you down, take them to the Lord in prayer and He who hears in secret will reward you openly. The path of life we choose for ourselves reflects our belief in our Triune God. God would that no one be lost, but that decision is up to you and up to me.

ACCORDING TO HIS PLAN

Through Jesus Christ God came to earth and wrapped Himself in human flesh and became as one of us.

When this truth we take in our souls jump for joy just as John leaped within his mother's womb when Mary visited Elisabeth before Jesus was born.

Our souls still get excited when in the middle of the night we wake up and contemplate spending eternity with our creator.

In the beginning Jesus created us out of the dust of the ground and within us put a vibrant soul, one attuned to the will of God.

Upon the demise of our bodies we will return to the dust of the ground and be blown about by a might wind, but God will not be in that wind, for our souls will be residing with Him.

Death will not be the end to life, just the opposite, death of the body will be the beginning of a new life.

A life more glorious than our feeble minds can comprehend, flesh unto flesh, spirit unto spirit, our eyes shall open to take in the glory of Almighty God.

Pray that we will learn our lessons well while on this blue planet we live, for beyond the distant horizon there is a life awaiting the obedient soul that we now cannot see.

Spend your time reading the Holy Scriptures, for within the pages thereof is the secret to eternal life and this secret will only be revealed to those who seek to do the will of God in their lives.

Forsake thy sinful past and seek the forgiveness of Jesus Christ and He will set thee free, free to wander the whole of His creation, not just the planet we now call home.

God through His Son Jesus Christ gave us life and gave Himself for the remission of our sins so that we might have life and have it more abundantly.

To help us navigate the shoals of sin Jesus gave us a guide to hold our hand in our times of need, the Holy Ghost is He, the third part of the trinity.

Fear not, for God the Father, God the Son and God the Holy Ghost will be with us forevermore, Jesus Christ opened the door to eternal life for those who turn from their evil ways and bow in submission before His throne, declaring that He (Jesus) is King of kings and Lord of lords.

What a glorious day it will be when our souls will hear God declare, "Welcome, come, enter eternity and live forever with me."

Through accepting Jesus Christ as our Lord and Savior our souls can rest in peace until our eyes close in death and we awaken to a new life, one where we will never again have to endure sin, disease, heartache, death, or pain.

Now is the time to forsake our sinful ways, now is the time to turn our lives over to Jesus Christ, now is the time to prepare for eternity, for our days are as a fleeting cloud, seen for a moment and then gone.

ALLOWING GOD TO SHAPE OUR LIVES

The Bible is the greatest book ever written, God inspired the writers of the Bible to put on paper His word, that it might be a guide of life to all who adhere to its teachings.

Whatever the problem the Bible has "The" answer, whatever the sin the Bible has the "Perfect" solution, whatever the disease the Bible has "The Perfect" cure, yes all solutions to the problems of mankind can be found in the Bible.

If for any reason one cannot find the solution to any given problem God will give us the endurance to live with that problem, for often times God allows discomfort in our lives in order to bring us closer to Him, but at no time will God put more on us than we are capable of handling.

Our loving triune God will never abandon us regardless of our circumstances, His love transcends all of mankind' problems and offers answers to any and all circumstances in which we might find ourselves, for neither life nor death can separate us from the love of God and His concern for our welfare.

God will allow us to go through circumstances so that later we will be equipped to help guide others through what we have already been through, at the time we may not like or appreciate what we might have to endure, but at sometime we will come to know why we had to endure what we did.

In other words God allows us to go through the fires of purification in order to burn off the dross and leave us as pure gold, gold that can be molded into whatever God wants so that we can be of service to him and our fellowman.

Tempered by adversity we become as a tool in God's hand to bring comfort to those in need and to bring hope where there is despair, while we ourselves grow in the knowledge of God and how He wants us to serve Him.

Looking back on our trials and tribulations we can clearly see why we had to go through them and how much we have to offer others, for God knows us better than we know ourselves and if we allow Him he will mold us into whatever serves his purpose rather than our own.

To completely submit to the will of God can be and often is a apprehensive experience, for one thing we do not think as God thinks and cannot see the end results as God sees them, we submit out of faith, not a blind faith, but the faith that we have in an all knowing and loving God, one who would not put us through anything that would bring harm of any kind to us.

In allowing God to shape our lives we are saying that we would rather serve God than to blunder through life without a purpose for life other than to satisfy our wants. God can and will supply all that we need to have a fulfilled life. With Him and through Him we can be an asset to the growth of God's kingdom here on earth. The greatest contribution we can make to that end is to submit to the will of God and allow Him to shape our lives.

AMONG THE FLOWERS

Walking in the garden among the flowers, I find solace
and tranquility.

In the garden of Gethsemane, I sense the anguish Jesus
felt the night He was betrayed.

At night when I bend my knees in prayer, I find security
in the knowledge that God is listening to me.

Before dawn, I search the eastern sky in hopes of seeing
the clouds gathering, anticipating Jesus' return.

During the heat of the day I recall the Exodus and the
hardships that Moses and his people had to face.

For forty years they wandered from place to place before
they crossed the Jordon and entered the land
of milk and honey.

In the cool of the evening I talk with God and confess my
daily sins, anticipating a peaceful night's sleep.

What I enjoy the most is the time among the flowers
communing with God and seeking His grace.

We like the flowers have our day in the sun and then it is
time to return to our maker so that our children can
have their time in the garden of life
among the flowers.

ARE YOU ONE OF THOSE?

Be not one of those who say, "I will wait until tomorrow to pray,
I do not have time today."

Be not one of those who say, "I will wait until tomorrow before I
seek his will; I do not have time today."

Be not one of those who say, "I will wait until tomorrow to give
myself to the Lord, I am too busy today."

Be not one of those who turn their back on the Lord and fall to
the temptations of sin.

All of those above will one day regret that they turned their back
on the Lord above.

Their earthly days may be full of the pleasures of sin, but the day
will come when it will crumble and come caving in.

Then will you hear them cry, "Save me O lord I pray. Save me and
I will be yours today."

With a tear in His eye and a frown on His face the Lord will answer,
"Sorry, I called you yesterday and you would not come. You
chose the pleasures of sin over Me, now you must pay."

"Save me O Lord, save me," they will cry. The Lord will reply, "Where
were you when I knocked? I tried, but you were too busy
trying to hide."

"Save me", they will cry one last time, and again the Lord will reply,
"I know thee not, be on your way."

As their voices fade away, it will be heard, "If only I had it to do over again, I would obey the Lord and avoid the penalties of my sins, please Lord, let me in."

As they fade from view they will hear, "Sorry you made your choice and refused to listen. Now you must share the fate of all who turn me away.

ARE YOU READY FOR A NEW LIFE

Are you resigned to the fact that one day you will die? Are you ready to die? Have you made peace with God? Did you do all you could to enhance the kingdom of God while you had the opportunity? Where will you go after death, heaven or hell? These questions and more have to be answered by all of us. God has allotted each of so many days here on earth and no matter how hard we might try, we can neither add days to our lives or take any away. God created us and set us free to do with our days here on earth whatever we choose for ourselves.

We are never too young to prepare ourselves for death, the more we understand about God and apply that knowledge to our lives the less likely we will be fearful about death. It takes a lifetime of preparation to be able to say, "I am ready". In our younger years, we see death as something that happens to the older generations, but death is no respecter of persons, it can come to anyone at any stage of life. Death is a part of life and all shall face their own death in due time and either embrace it with the conviction that there is life after the death of the body or fear death because we are unprepared for it and have put material things before spiritual matters.

One way of looking at death is seeing life as a butterfly. Before a butterfly became a butterfly it went through a metamorphosis stage where a caterpillar wove a cocoon around itself, while inside of this cocoon, it was changed and came out of the cocoon transformed into a beautiful butterfly. Before we became a child of God, we went through a metamorphosis stage where we wrapped ourselves in the teachings of the Holy Scriptures (cocoon), while in this process we were changed and emerged from our cocoon a beautiful child of God.

Death is a means by which we can leave this life and all its problems behind and enter into a new life in the presence of God, one prepared for those who have turned their lives over to the will of God and prepared themselves for such a transition. Those who have traversed this life without preparing for what lies beyond the grave will be denied entrance into the kingdom of God, instead they will be cast from God's sight forever and ever. We become as that beautiful child of God or we become a lost sinner.

While on earth, the followers of Jesus Christ and the unrepentant sinners feed together, are watered by the rains of heaven, and grow to maturity, upon death the followers of Jesus Christ are separated from the unrepentant sinners. The followers of Jesus Christ pass through the pearly gates and enter into heaven, whereas the unrepentant sinners are cast from God' sight and spend eternity tormented in the fires of hell. We ourselves determine where we will send eternity by who we follow while here on earth, God or Satan.

Our life here on earth is as the mist of early morning, when the sun rises over the horizon the mist dissipates and is seen on more. Now is the time to choose where we will spend eternity, we have today but before the break of another day death may over take us and then it will be too late to change or choose where we will spend eternity. We will be judged by God and His judgment will be just, there will be wailing and gnashing of teeth.

ARE YOU READY TO DIE

When the sunset of life comes, will you be ready and equipped to face death and the life beyond the grave? The Bible admonishes us to put our life in order and thereby be prepared for eternity. Many are too busy trying to fulfill their dreams and ambitions to be concerned about spiritual matters and put off these preparations with the argument that they will have plenty of time later to worry about such things. The problem with this kind of thinking is that one does not know the day of their demise, only God know this. God does not promise us tomorrow nor does he promise us that we will have plenty of time to prepare for death and what lies beyond the grave. Not to prepare for death and life beyond the grave is like leaving your house unlocked in a bad neighborhood where crime runs rampant and hoping no one will break in and steal. As we can take steps against theft, so can we take steps against the day of death to assure that we will be ready for life beyond the grave.

In our youth, we think that nothing is going to harm us and dying is for the elderly. Death does not respect age nor does it care if we are ready or not. Many just run and play through life without a care, just as long as they can fulfill their earthly desires they are seemingly happy. They disregard their spiritual life under the guise that they have plenty of time or that they do not believe in God. They are spoiled in the luxuries of this world and raise their children in the same way. When their day to leave this life comes, they are completely unprepared and often make false confessions as to their beliefs in hopes of avoiding any possibility of accountability for how they lived their lives.

Our children live with us for such a short period of time, they deserve all of the love and respect that we can give them. This does not mean to spoil them for in doing so they will not be prepared to live on their own and having the skills to earn a living and the resources to support themselves. Discipline is essential when raising children; it may seem like harsh punishment at the time but when grown they will thank you for loving them enough to discipline them when young. The old adage of spare the rod and spoil the child is just as relevant today as when it was first used. Raise a child in the way that he should go and when he is old, he will not depart from his ways. Discipline through love produces respect in return.

Through the verses of the Bible, we learn that it would be better if we were never born than to hurt one of these little ones, for such is the kingdom of God and we must become as little children before we can enter the kingdom of God.
Jesus spoke in parables, thus hiding the meaning that He wanted to get across, through study and prayer we come to know the hidden meaning of what He was saying. It is advantageous to put aside what we are doing and study Jesus and His teaching and apply them to our lives and by so doing we grow closer to Jesus and reflect his teachings in our

lives. Thus making us better parents and having the tools by which we can discipline our offspring in a more loving way, thus preparing them to face life's problems in the light of scripture.

God does not need man to be complete, but man needs God to be complete. The more we study the life and teachings of Jesus Christ the more answers we find to everyday life problems and the better understanding we have of what the purpose of this life is. The primary purpose of this life is to come to a better understanding of God, what He wants for our lives and applying His will to our lives and to prepare us for life after death. The scriptures have the answers to all of life's problems and are there to guide us through this life. We are not ready to live until we are ready to die.

In the final days, the tares (unrepentant souls) shall be separated from the wheat (followers of Christ) and be cast into the fires of hell. This life is where we become a follower of Jesus Christ or a follower of Satan and this is by what we believe and how we apply these beliefs to our lives. Our place in God's kingdom is ours to claim, but we have to prepare ourselves now, before we close our eyes in death. We control our own destiny and are responsible for our own actions and by these actions, we shall be judged.

There are two doors, which we can walk through after death, one door leads to heaven and the other leads to hell, our decisions here and now determine which door will be open to us. One door or the other is opened by the way that we live and conduct ourselves in this life.

ARE YOU READY?

Are you prepared to pass through the door of death and into the presence of God?

Have you done your homework and passed the test of life?

Has God put you through the fires of life and burned all of the dross away?

Have you surrendered your life to Jesus Christ and conformed your way of life to His will?

Is your life so precious that you do not want to give it up and receive a more rewarding life?

When will it be, when will you come to realize that death is a part of living and that all life here on earth will one day come to an end?

Do you know that there is life beyond what we call death and that there is only two places where we will spend eternity, either with God or in hell?

Questions, more questions than answers, or at least it seems that way.

There is a place where one can find answers to all of their questions about life and that is at the foot of the cross, the cross where our Lord and Savior,

Jesus Christ, gave His life for the remission of your sins and mine.

Give up your quest for earthly riches and fame, rather seek the will of God in your life and you will find that life does have a meaning that goes beyond the riches of this world, for the things of this world are temporal, while the things of God are forever and will never change.

Preparing for life beyond the grave should be the quest of all while there is still day, for once death knocks on our door it is too late to seek that straight and narrow road that leads to eternal life, by this time we have already decided where we want to spend eternity, by doing nothing we condemn ourselves to hell.

By following Jesus' teachings as found in the Holy Scriptures we prepare ourselves for life beyond the grave, a life that awaits all who give up earthly quests and seeks the will of God in their lives.

It is your decision, it is my decision as to how we live our lives, and God will never interfere in the way that we live, for we are free moral agents, free to choose how we want to spend our days here on earth, by the same token we shall be held responsible for our decisions and if we choose to live outside of God's will we will face eternity in hell, live within the confines of God's will and live forever in His presence.

In the end, after we have passed from this life all of our questions about life here on earth will be answered and we will have no excuses for living outside of the will of God, for the evidence of God's love and forgiveness is with us every day of our lives and can be seen in all that we observe.

Evil (Satan) is a powerful force in this world and Satan is relentless in his quest to get us to follow the ways of the world rather than the ways of God, he is the prince of this world, not the king, just the prince.

Like all of us he will one day submit and declare that God is supreme and in complete control of all things, great and small, and will submit to God whether he wants to or not, God has prepared a special place for all who do not submit to His will, a place that no one in his right mind wants to spend eternity.

But rather come to God before death and accept His Son Jesus Christ as your Lord and Savior and you will inherit eternal life, this is one of the promises of the Bible and what God declares as the truth will remain the truth forever and ever.

AT THE END OF LIFE

My bed of joy is empty, my youth has passed, and
old age is all that is left.

Thoughts of love have turned to thoughts of death,
where will my soul rest, in paradise
or in hell?

When I was young I never dreamed that one day I
would have to face my past and try to justify how I
lived this life God gave to me.

Through the trials of life I have come to question
not my Lord and my God, for He is great and I am
but a child of perdition.

I have known His never ending Love and He has
guided me all the days of my life, I now await the
grave and the life beyond.

My eyes have grown dim, my flesh was once like
silken cloth, now it is wrinkled and worn with
time.

My thoughts wander as I dream of love as I knew
it in my youth, now my body responds not; I smile
and return to sleep till the break of dawn.

Man of sorrows am I, where once I was full of life,
now the pangs of death beseech me and soon I will
succumb to this way of life.

O where O where have the years gone, from youth
to old age is but the wink of an eye, all things
change and yet they remain the same.

Though I fear not death I long for the days of old
when my eyes were sharp and I could hear the call
of the wild, now all I hear is the rustling of deaths
door.

O Lord God grant me eternal life as I walk through
the door of death, into Thy hands I commend my
soul, that I might look upon Thy face and rejoice
in Thy presence forevermore.

AWAITING JESUS' RETURN

How Long Lord Jesus, how long before your return, we gaze skyward in anticipation of the clouds gathering in the East to herald your return. Signs of you return become more apparent day-by-day, world events suggest that the time is near. We look forward to the culmination of the events that are foretold in the scriptures and once again, you will walk among your created beings and be a "Light" unto our path.

As we walk our pathway of life we search the horizon for signs of your return, just the thought brings joy to our hearts and peace to our soul. The shackles that bind us will fall away, leaving us free of the cares of this world, changing our life and lifestyle to one that pleases Thee. Anxiously we scan the skies, looking for the clouds that will reveal Thee, Lord Jesus come and free us from our earthly bonds.

We are anxious to see the new home You have prepared for us in Your father's kingdom where we will no longer live in fear of tomorrow. Where we will be free to soar with the angels, drink of the waters of the fountain of life, and live forever with Thee. Peace and love will reign where once strife prevailed; no longer will the dark clouds of sin stand in our way. When we reach out to Thee O Lord Your love burns within us, it sooths our fevered brow and wipes all of our fears away.

When we enter the twilight of life and our eyes become dim, our hearts will be filled with joy with the thoughts of living with You for eternity. Many desire to be with You Lord Jesus, but only those who choose to bow before Your throne and accept that You are the one and only Son of God will be allowed to enter therein. We stand before Your door and knock Lord, open it and let us in, that we might glorify Thee.

You are the Good Shepherd who seeks the lost sheep, that they might see Thy loving face, hear Your voice in the wilderness of this lost world, respond to Your soothing voice, and find peace of soul. We, the lost sheep, humble ourselves before Thy throne, seeking forgiveness of our sins, cleansed in Thy shed blood of Calvary, waiting for Thy return.

BE AS A "LIGHT" UNTO THE WORLD

May the word of our loving God flow over the land like a healing balm and heal the disquieted soul and comfort the broken hearted.

May His word water the thirsty soul and bring forth the fruit of salvation among those who bow their heads before His throne.

Waters that run deep and sustains the vegetation that covers the land are like jewels given out of love for ones mate, for without life sustaining water surly the land would dry up and be as a desert in the midst of trying times.

God is faithful and will not turn His head from those who earnestly seek to do His will, He will sustain them with manna from heaven as He did His people when He lead them out of bondage in the land of Egypt.

Trust in God to supply all of your needs and you will never go without, for He is faithful to care for all who love Him and trust Him for their needs.

Those who step forth in faith and share their relationship with God with others will be rewarded with eternal bliss when they pass from this world and stand with humbleness before the great white throne of God.

Be as the waters of this world that nourish God's creation, nourish ye the hearts of your fellowman as he seeks change in his life, not by you, but by the knowledge of God that is within you.

An encouraging word can bring one to the foot of the cross, criticism can drive one away, be as refreshing water that brings new life to all who partake thereof and may your well of love for your fellowman never run dry.

Spread the seed of the word of God, let another water with encouragement and at harvest time let God reap the harvest, for it is by Him and through Him that we ourselves were saved.

Be a part of God's great plan for His creation by living your life in the "Light" of the one who created us all, let not the shadow of sin keep you from your rightful place in His kingdom, a kingdom reserved for all who turn to God and strive to drink of the waters of eternal life.

Be as a "Light" set upon a hill, may your relationship with God be an inspiration to those whom you come in contact with, water God's creation with love and compassion that has been shown to you, thus fulfilling the calling to which you have been called.

BE GRATEFUL

Hold me Lord, hold me by the hand and lead me in the way that you want me to go.

O Lord that I might exemplify Thee while I am here and may I enjoy that which You have prepared for me.

Let not the dark hours and the storms of life overwhelm me, that I might be a tool for good in Thy hands.

May I reflect Thy love and be a friend to my fellow man, all are walking in the darkness of sin, searching for the "Light" that comes from Thee.

You are God; we are but wandering souls in the desert of sin, in search of eternal life.

Just as You have power to create, so do You have the power to release us from the bondage of sin.

We are not worthy of Thy love O Lord, but we seek Thee still, we seek the comfort that you bring to all who obey Your will.

That all become as one and sing praises unto Thy Holy name and may our praise be worthy of Thine ear.

Even thou we sin O Lord, keep us from falling into the great abyss, it is only through You O Lord that we are able to withstand the sins of the world.

Lord of lords, King of kings, You are all that there is, You stand before all as a refuge for those who seek shelter from the storms of life.

Be ever mindful that gratitude comes from the soul, not the tongue, the tongue will say what it has to deceive those near, God looks upon the heart and rewards accordingly.

BEFORE THY TABLE

As I kneel before thy table O Lord, wash me white as snow.

Cleanse me of all un-righteousness; renew my thoughts so that I might serve You with a contrite and upright heart.

May I see beyond self and be a friend to my fellow man.

Purge me of my sins O Lord; wipe my tears away so that I might see thee more clearly.

As I partake of the sacraments of thy table, I feel thy Love surge through my veins.

As I drink of thy blood O Lord, it quenches the thirst of my soul and I become more like thee.

As I eat of thy body O Lord, my hunger for thy word is fulfilled.

I do these things in remembrance of thee O Lord; I humble myself in thy presents and accept thy will.

I stand in awe of thy sacrifice for a poor sinner such as me.

I seek thy forgiveness, as before thy table I kneel.

Cleanse me Lord; cleanse my body so that one day my soul might return unto thee, for this is where I seek to be.

BEHOLD THE GLORY OF HEAVEN

1 Corinthians 2:9 But as it is written, Eye hath not seen, nor ear heard, neither have entered into the heart of man, the things which God hath prepare for them that love Him.

One day like a butterfly, we will emerge from our human cocoon and take wing in the presence of Almighty God. We will soar like an eagle on the wind. With eyes that will take in everything.

In awe and wonder, we will make our way towards the great throne of God; there we will cast our wreath of life before Him. His voice will be like peals of thunder and yet we will understand every word that will proceed out His mouth.

With bowed head, we will submit to His authority and worship Him as never before. Our hearts will burn with the fire of His love and our eyes will behold the glory of His countenance as upon His great throne He sits in judgment of our earthly lives.

Round about Him we will see the vastness and beauty of His heavenly realm. Beauty and landscapes beyond our description will lie before us, all for us to enjoy. This will be our new home, one made without hands, never to succumb to the temptations of Satan again.

We will run like the wind and not be tired. We will have boundless energy, renewed by the fruit of the trees that bear their fruit every month. Our new bodies will never again know pain, disease or death again.

His radiance will be the "Light" of our new home. Never will darkness or storm threaten us again. His "Light" will shine from one end of heaven to the other, lighting our way as we take in the majesty of His heavenly creation.

He will talk with us, His voice will comfort us, and His countenance will be as a shining "Light", we will fear Him not, for His message to us will be as a message of love from a father to his child.

All fear will be gone and we will stand tall and hold our heads high as we go about our tasks that are for the benefit of all. No one will hold anything back or try to hide and keep something for him or herself. God's abundance will be everywhere and shared by all.

We cannot even begin to describe or comprehend what heaven will be like, but we can prepare ourselves for the transition from our earthly life to our eternal life by studying the Holy Scriptures and accepting God's Son, Jesus Christ, as our Lord and Savior. This will be our new home, prepared not by hands but by the word of God.

BEWARE OF TEMPTATIONS

As I walk the pathway of life, I cannot see the pitfalls that will besiege me. I can only walk by faith and trust in the Lord.

Many times, I will stumble and partake of the forbidden fruit. It will be sweet in my mouth, but in the end, it will be bitter in my belly.

Only by calling upon the name of the Lord will I be able to overcome. The ways of sin are very deceiving and reveals not the death that can follow.

Satan is the great deceiver and will not reveal his intentions until we are under his spell, then it will take the understanding of God's word to overcome.

Test all temptations against the word of God and if it does not comply turn from it, seek the shelter of God's wing, and hold fast to His word.

God will provide a way out of every temptation; never will He leave us alone (even though at the time it may seem that way) to struggle by ourselves.

Read the Holy Scriptures and commit the truths found there to memory so that when Satan tempts you to stray you can say, "I am a child of God, go your way" and Satan will flee.

I repeat; test all temptations against the word of God, for where you spend eternity depends upon it. Satan is out to destroy you. God's word can keep your soul from going to hell.

BEYOND THE CROSS

Beyond the cross, Jesus still lives, vibrant as ever, waiting
for you and me to join Him in Paradise.

Beyond the cross, there is only the ever presence now with
no more earthly cares.

Beyond the cross, there is no more sin, disease nor death,
just peace and tranquility.

Beyond the cross, are the martyrs of the past, James being
the first, and all of the rest who gave their lives for
the advancement of God's kingdom here
on earth.

Beyond the cross, there are the streets of gold, the tree of
life and sights beyond our imagination.

Beyond the cross, the book of life with the names of the
ones who accepted Jesus Christ as their Lord
and Savior.

Beyond the cross, Jesus calling to the sheep of His pasture
to come and share what he has for those who love Him.

Beyond the cross, Jesus waits to see if you and I accept His
invitation to join Him in Paradise. I have, have you?

Beyond the cross, the sheep hear their Masters voice calling
them to join Him in singing praises unto God
and saying, A-men.

BEYOND TOMORROW

There is a day a-coming beyond tomorrow that has no
end or any sorrow.

Lord Jesus has it ready for those who believe that He
is who He claims to be.

There is no sun by day, nor moon by night, for Jesus
is its "Light".

The flowers, trees and grasses that grow along the way
will dazzle the eyes, their beauty will never
fade away.

The streams run cool and deep, from the throne of God
they flow and run out of sight.

Their waters are for the healing of the nations, their
banks they will never overflow.

Unlike the floods of Egypt, their waters bring only joy
and delight.

There are no wild beasts to cause any fright, just those
who graze upon the sweet grasses and rest
each night.

There is a day beyond tomorrow that has no end or any
sorrow.

A rainbow forms the gate that leads to this day beyond
tomorrow and only the pure in heart can pass
through it.

The Great Shepherd is waiting for His sheep to pass through
that gate and leave behind all who are contrite
and full of fright.

Only a chosen few who are pure in heart and full of God's
Light will be allowed to enter this new day beyond
tomorrow that has no end or any sorrow.

BOAT OF LIFE

As I row my boat of life the storm clouds gather and
the seas run high.

The breaking seas run high and threaten to flood my
boat of life with sin, thus engulfing me.

I grab my bailer and one scoop at a time I throw my
sins at the feet of the one who can save
me, Jesus Christ.

As I row against the tide of life, I come across a few
who row by my side and avoid getting
caught in the whirlpool of sin.

The row is hard, but for those who survive the rewards
refresh the soul and they too get to anchor
in the bay of God's love.

Through the darkness of night, I steer my boat of life by
the "Light" of God from above.

When the fog is thick and I cannot see I listen for His
voice to guide me.

From out of the fog I hear His voice say, "Follow Me and
I will see you home safe this day."

As the years passed, I came to recognize the signs along
life's way, some read, "Beware, sin ahead", others
say, "Stay the course and reap your
just rewards."

When the sun sets on life those who have rowed their Boat
of Life by the Bright and Morning Star (Jesus Christ)
will enter a snug harbor and ride at anchor on
the tranquil sea of Eternity.

CAN IT BE
SAID OF YOU

Have you done what you came to earth to do, or have
you turns your head and left it up to someone
else to do?

Did God call you to do something for Him and you
said, "Not me Lord, for I know not what to say
or do."

Lest you forget, it was God who created you, don't
you think you owe Him a thing or two?

As for me, I sure do, without Him, I do not know
what I would do.

He loves us and wants us to know that all He wants
is a chance to make His word come to life
through you and me.

Without you and me, He wouldn't have a representative
through which He can give a helping hand to
those in need.

Lay self aside and do what God has called you to do,
let not another day go by, for tomorrow you
may die, then when you stand before
His throne you will have to
explain why you did not
do what He called
you to do.

Whatever your calling God will see that you have all
that you need to tell your story to those in
need to what you have to say or do.

It will be a turning point in your life, a life that was
once mundane will turn into a life of servitude.

Serving God will brighten your days when you reach
out beyond your families and friends, you can
make a difference in the lives of
those in need.

Hold not back from serving God, lest He cast you aside
when this earth you leave, for as sure as you were
born, one day God will call you home and
then what will you do if you have said,
"Not me Lord."

God will not ask forever for you to serve Him, He will
allow you to do as you please, but wouldn't it be
better to serve God than one day to hear
Him say, "Sorry, you turned your head
from Me, now I turn My head
from you."

CAST THY CROWNS BEFORE THE THRONE OF GOD

Whatever we do in life, whatever greatness we may accomplish, whomever we may help along the way, remember that it was through the love of God that we were given the talent to accomplish the things that we want out of life.

We may not recognize that it was by God's love and grace that we were able to accomplish our goals in life and we may not give thanks to God for the ability to fulfill those goals. Then stop and consider that without God's love, grace and guidance none of our accomplishments would have been fulfilled.

It was God who set us on the path of life and it was God who put into our thoughts the things that He wanted us to accomplish and it is God whom we should bow your head before and give thanks for our successes in life.

With and through God all things are possible, listen for that still small voice as you go about your daily tasks. Listen and obey and our life's journey will be more fulfilling than what the things of this world can ever offer.

We are called to rise above life's trials and accomplishments and cast our crowns before the throne of God, boast not of ourselves or our accomplishments, for without God and His love for us none of them would have come to fruition.

Put self aside, lest our boasting leads to self-centeredness and we lose sight of where our loyalties lay. Humble ourselves before the throne of God and cast our crowns before His throne, for all glory, honor and praise belongs to God.

The humble heart is a willing heart in the eyes of God and it is these whom God calls upon to accomplish His will here on earth. Others may volunteer, but if their heart is not right with God He will turn them aside and allow them to wallow in their own self-righteousness. Their reward will be here in this world whereas the humble in heart will lay up treasures in heaven where neither moth nor rust can destroy.

This world is a place of preparation for the life to come after the death of the body. It is also a place to choose whether we want to serve God or serve our own self-interests. God gave us a free will to do as we see fit for ourselves. It is up to each one to choose between doing the will of God in our lives or falling prey to the temptations of Satan. The Scriptures make it very clear that we either serve God or serve Satan. The two cannot co-exist nor can we serve both.

We either cast our crowns before the throne of God or cast them at the feet of Satan. Which one have you chosen?

CHOICES

Every day of our lives, we make choices; some affect our way of living while others affect our spiritual life. Through choices, we reflect what is important in our lives. Choosing to put materialism foremost in our lives and ignoring our spiritual life puts us in danger of damnation in the respect we put more value on materialism than we do on our spiritual life, thus leaving ourselves vulnerable to the temptations of Satan and ultimately separation from God for eternity.

Satan is very subtle in how he presents his temptations and is often seen as a shining light, this is when all temptations should be exposed to the truths as found in the Holy Scriptures and if found wanting disregard them, if found valid them expand on them. Choices like these can and do have a profound effect on our lives and how we live. To follow Satan even though it seems right or will enhance our way of living is no more than giving Satan permission to influence our lives and lead us astray, which is his goal.

Even though ensnared by Satan's temptations it is not impossible to escape them. The struggle may be difficult but we can overcome temptations through devotion to and turning one's life over to God. Through the Holy Scriptures, one can learn of and apply the truths of God to their lives. It may be a long arduous journey but whatever effort it will take, will pay off in the end. The choice to change one's life for the better is the first step in becoming a child of God, when we do our part God will do His. Change may come slowly or it may be instantaneous, but either way it will be the beginning of the greatest adventure of one's life.

All choices are personal, one cannot make choices for another, we can encourage others to make good choices but we cannot force them to do so. Enlightened by the scriptures and encouragement can change one's life and lifestyle. Changing for the better and turning your life over to God does not in any way imply that one will gain financially or socially, it does however guarantee that you will live a life more pleasing to God and find a peace and love that you have never experienced before. It also opens up an avenue of help in making everyday decisions and choices about all aspects of life.

It is one's choice as to whom they want to follow, God or Satan. This choice is one that no one can avoid, and by doing nothing, one automatically accepts Satan and his ways as their goal. This choice is one that eventually leads to eternal death, separated from God forever in a place commonly referred to as hell. The choice to follow God requires studying the Holy Scriptures and applying the truths therein to one's life and accepting God's Son, Jesus Christ, as their Lord and Savior.

We will never be perfect or always make the best of choices but we will have the knowledge of where to find information that will guide us in our decision and choice making process. Through prayer and supplication, we can live our lives in peace with the choices that we make and have a safe haven where we can find guidance and help in our times of need. Only through Jesus Christ, can we come to the redeeming grace of God and make choices pleasing to Him.

CHRISTIAN FOLLOW ME

Jesus calls across the centuries, "Christians, forsake thy wicked ways and follow Me."

When Satan tempts you to stray, tell him "I haven't time to listen to you. All I have time for is to pray."

Jesus tells us that if Satan persists that we have His permission to use His name against him. If we listen to Satan, he will lead us astray and when he is done with us, he will abandon us and leave us to die in our sins.

Satan is sadistic, selfish and full of greed, clever is he when it comes to deceiving those who live life as they please.

Pleasure of the flesh is but for a moment, when it is through it leaves you empty inside. Fulfilling the desires of lust leads to nothing but heartache and pain.

Sugar coated temptations may be sweet in the mouth, but when reality sets in they turn bitter in your belly leaving you empty inside with no place to go except to hell and Satan will laugh at you all of the way.

Satan may be the Prince of this world along with those angels who chose to follow him, but the day is coming when they will be bound by the truths of God and thrown into the bottomless pit. There they will remain for a thousand years.

During this time, Jesus will restore peace and harmony throughout this world. Peace and harmony that heretofore we have only dreamed of will become a reality, a prelude of what is to come.

One last time Satan and his fallen angels will be released from the bottomless pit just before they are thrown into the lake of fire where the worm never dies. There he and all who followed him will be tormented forever and ever. Never again, to interfere in the lives of those who chose to follow Jesus Christ.

Now you know the rest of the story. A sad story indeed, but one that will come true for all who point their finger at God and say, "I do not need you nor your Son, Jesus Christ or the Holy Spirit in my life. Go away and leave me alone."

CONFUSING?

In the new world to come there will be no more time as we know it now, no yesterday, no today and no tomorrow, just the ever present now. Though our eyes are open and we can hear, we are both blind and deaf as concerning of what lies ahead of us, it is beyond our comprehension or ability to understand. Just the thought of there being no more time is enough to disturb most people.

Man's conception of the new heaven and new earth has to be on a human level in order for man to even begin to understand any of it. The Bile describes the new world as being fifteen hundred miles long, fifteen hundred miles wide and fifteen hundred miles in height and that the walls thereof are seventy two yards by man' measure. A question comes to mind, how many spirits (people) can one put into a world that size? Does the spirit man take up less space than we as humans do or does he take up any space at all? There is a river running through the middle of it with trees on both sides that yield their fruit every month. How can this be in such a small area when our earthly world is many times fifteen hundred miles square and humans are overcrowding it?

There are many more questions about the new heaven and the new earth than man has answers for. In fact, man knows very little about the new heaven and the new earth. All he knows is what God wants him to know, because God knows that man in his present state can in no way comprehend the spiritual world except to know that it is a much better place to live than the material world that he now lives in. We will only find the answers about the new world to come when we leave this life behind and enter into the spiritual world that exists beyond our earthly existence. Only then will we be able to witness to its beauty and fullness thereof, for the present we must accept its beauty and fullness thereof by faith. Faith in that which we now cannot see nor touch and this being through our faith in Jesus Christ, the Son of God.

God has allowed us to know just enough about the new world to come so that we can know what a glorious life we have to look forward to. As He has told us, He has created all things for His pleasure, and that includes you and me. When we finally experience this new heaven and new earth, we will enjoy all that He has prepared for those who love Him.

There will be no more confusion and all of our questions will be answered to the satisfaction of all, for God will hold nothing back from us and content we will be as we go about our newly appointed tasks. One of which will be to be in constant praise for what God has done for us through His Son, Jesus Christ.

DEATH IS INEVITABLE

Just as man was born into a new life so will he die to a new life. God knew us before we were conceived in our mother's womb, and when we die we will once again be in His presence. We will be judged for how we lived our lives here on earth and accordingly be assigned our permanent residence, heaven or hell. We ourselves determine our own destiny by the choices that we make throughout our lifetime.

Many have a fear of death and yet death is a part of living, every living soul here on earth one day will embrace death and personally find out that, there is life after the death of the body. The statement has been made that the only thing that we have to fear is fear itself. Once fear of death is conquered then death is seen as a natural process of life and holds no mystery or fear for those who come to believe and know that Jesus Christ is the door to eternal life.

God created man to live forever in the Garden of Eden, but through the disobedience of Adam and Eve when they partook of the forbidden fruit, they introduced the phenomenon that we know as death. If it were not for this, man would live forever in his present state, but due to the sin that was introduced through disobedience man has to go through the process of death to separate his soul from his sin-contaminated flesh. Neither flesh nor sin can enter into the kingdom of God. It will only be through Jesus Christ that man will receive a new body, one free from the incumbencies of this life, especially sin.

There is a story in the Bible that tells of a rich man who died and went to hell, in hell he was tormented day and night. He beseeched his tormentors to allow him to return to his brothers and warn them that if they did not change their ways that they too would end up in hell. But was informed that his brothers had Moses and the Prophets and if they did not listen to them then they would not believe one who returned from the dead. So it is with us of today, if we do not believe the scriptures, neither would we believe one who returned from the dead. We have already had one return from the dead, Jesus Christ, He rose from the dead and made Himself known to many and yet there are those who do not believe.

The first death (death of the body) is not to be feared nor can it be avoided; rather it is to be embraced as being part of life and as a door to life beyond the grave. The second death is the one to be feared, it is reserved for those who reject Jesus Christ and pursue the things of this world without regard for life after death. These are those who will be cast from God's sight and spend eternity tormented in the fires of hell. God gives us free choice as to how we live our lives and by our choices we will be judged, no one is exempt from His authority over our final destination, heaven or hell.

DO NOT BE DECEIVED BY SATAN

Satan has many ways of deceiving the unsuspecting and making his ways appear right and just. He clouds the mind of man with the gifts that he offers and once accepted he springs the trap of deception. Satan is without a doubt still alive and well. He can appear as a shining light with a mask of humbleness and sometimes he comes right to the point of what he wants us to do. Along with these demands, he can make the urge to do his bidding so powerful that it would be easier to obey him than to resist him. Nevertheless resist him we must and it can take all of our strength and fortitude not to succumb to his demands.

Satan is behind everything that does not reflect the truths of God. He can even twist these truths to present himself as an ambassador of good will. When in fact he has devious plans for whoever will succumb to his calling. Some of his biggest temptations consist of the promise of power, positions in high places, wealth, murder, control over others, anything that will keep us from seeking God and His righteousness.

God has cast Satan and one third of the angels out of heaven because of their revolt against God, never to be in His presence again. Satan is a liar and the father of all lies, and a deceiver. God stripped him of all of his heavenly powers and put him on a leash, he can go only so far and no further. God cast him and his fallen angels unto earth with only the power of deception. Satan cannot take the life of anyone, nor can he force anyone to do something against his or her will. Satan is the cause of all wars, unrest, anything that will cause man to turn against his fellowman. Satan is evil through and through. Satan will stay here on earth until the second coming of our Lord and Savior, Jesus Christ. Then he will be cast into the bottomless pit along with his fallen angels and peace will reign on earth for a thousand years and after that he will be loosed for a season and then cast into the lake of fire and there along with all who follow him will anguish in hell for eternity.

Satan knows that his time here on earth is short and he goes around like a roaring lion deceiving and devouring all who fall prey to his temptations. All who call upon the name of Jesus Christ and use the truths of God against Satan can overcome his temptations, where the "Light" of truth (Jesus Christ) shines evil cannot exist. Satan will flee for there is no truth in him and he cannot prevail against the truths of God as found in the Holy Scriptures. This is our weapon against Satan, store the truths of God in your heart and call upon them in your times of temptations and you shall prevail in your battle against evil.

It is a spiritual battle that we fight here on earth, a battle between good and evil. A battle that has been going on ever since Adam and Eve disobeyed God in the Garden of Eden when they partook of the fruit of the tree of the knowledge of good and evil. This battle will continue until the second coming of Jesus Christ. It is then and only then that we will be free from the influence of Satan. It is and will continue to be a constant struggle to keep from being deceived and falling victim to the evil ways of Satan. Jesus came to earth and paid the price for our sins (evil ways of Satan) through the shedding of His blood on the cross of Calvary. He and He alone holds the key to eternal life and He will give it to all who accept Him as their Lord and Savior.

DO NOT BE DECEIVED

Store the truths of God in thine heart, when troubled times come turn to them and hold them dear so that no one can deceive you lest you become lost and lose your way.

As the morning sun awakens a sleeping world may the word of God protect you from the jackals that lie in wait to devour the un-repentant heart.

Clouds of sin may obscure the word of God, but sin cannot keep the searching heart from learning the truth and living accordingly.

By night, pray according to the scriptures and by day walk the path of faith that lies before you.

Beware of those who profess to be followers of Jesus Christ and live by a different set of rules, they are as wolves in sheep's clothing trying to lead you astray and keep you from your Savior's side.

They are disciples of the evil one, their mouths are full of guile, deceit is in their eyes, hate of God is in their heart, they have learned from the father of all lies, Satan.

Even though their words please the flesh, test their utterances against the word of God and if it follows not the scriptures then turn from it lest you die.

Truth will never deceive, neither will it lead you down the wrong path, its "Light" will light your path and lead you through the minefields of deception.

In the end, truth and those who follow the truth will be left standing when the day of judgment comes, all others will be cast from God's sight and reap the harvest of deception.

Pray for the wisdom to discern the lies that are spread by Satan, live by the truth that is revealed in the Holy Scriptures and God will dwell in your heart all of your days.

Praise the Lord for His truth and saving grace, put all other things aside and live a life pleasing to God and you will never have to fear where you will spend eternity.

Heaven is the goal of all who accept God's one and only Son, Jesus Christ as their Lord and Savior, all others will be cast from God's sight forever and ever to suffer the consequences of their choice of rejecting the Son of God.

FENCES

Some are made of wood, stone, steel, concrete or various other materials.

Some high, some low, some topped with barbwire, some fences are self imposed, some with gates that swing just one way.

Some keep you in; some keep you out, for protection from wildlife, some are barriers to our growth, spiritual fences protect us from evil.

Spiritual fences consist of the truths at taught by Jesus Christ. These fences are built by and maintained by our faith in our Triune God.

They cannot be crossed by Satan or eroded by his evil ways, these fences had their foundations laid from the beginning of time.

A fence was put up by God when He told Satan, "This far and no further."

A fence built by Jesus, his sheep gather inside, protected by His love.

Jesus calls his sheep by name and they answer every time, offering them peace beyond understanding.

Within Jesus' fences we leave all earthly cares behind and and obey His every word, for only He has the key to eternal life.

Fences made by God last forever, fences made by man are
but for a short while, then they decay and are no more.

Cleave to the Lord; wander not from His pathways, gladly
enter into His sheepfold where His fences offer
protection from the ravaging wolves that
seek to devour all who stray.

FOOTPRINTS

May my footprints be light upon this earth and yet
distinct enough for others to follow.

May my voice be soft and yet may it be heard above
the shouts of sin.

May my ears hear the cries of my fellowman and may
I comfort them in their times of need.

May my hands toil for the kingdom of God and produce
fruit fit for God's table.

May my tongue utter words of praise instead of
condemnation.

May my legs be strong enough to carry me to the foot of
the cross where my Lord died and freed me from
the bondage of sin.

May my eyes see beyond the cross and bring my soul into
conformity with the love Jesus showed towards all.

May my arms embraced my fellowman when through the
trials of life we walk hand in hand.

May my pen spread the word of God to my fellowman and
make a difference in their lives.

To this end I commit my life to the advancement of God's
kingdom here on earth.

I thank God for all of the blessings that He has bestowed
upon me and for the privilege of allowing me to
be a part of His plan for mankind.

FREE AT LAST

We (you and I) are in complete control of our own destiny, when in adverse situations we have to make some hard decisions, to continue to follow the path that can lead to self-destruction or whether we are willing to make the necessary changes in our lifestyle to avoid such a fate. The biggest decision to make is to whether to follow the ways of Jesus Christ or the ways of Satan.

When we find ourselves hooked on drugs, alcohol, or a life of crime it can be hard to make the necessary changes that will free us our addiction. They offer relief from our real problems and once hooked on an addiction they can become a way of life and we become blinded to what we are doing to ourselves. Often we give up our families, a good job, our social life and more importantly our relationship with God. Many fall prey to an addiction to the point of and including death.

When a family member or a friend tries to intervene they strike back by telling them to keep out of their affairs, that they know what they are doing and can quit whenever they want and who are you to tell me how to live, you are no better than I am. With this attitude, the addiction goes unabated until finally they come to see the error of their ways or become a statistic, the choice is theirs.

The one who is addicted blames their problems on everyone else but themselves and falls deeper and deeper into their addiction, unwilling to change. They have allowed themselves to come under the control of Satan and do not realize that Satan now controls their life. Blinded by the false security of an addiction leads to self-destruction and this is Satan's ultimate goal of destroying all of God's creative beings that he can before he himself is cast into the lake of fire. It saddens the heart to watch a friend or family member succumb to an addiction and there is nothing you can do about it.

Intervention on behalf of the one who is addicted will offer them a chance to reform, but if it is not in their heart to do so then the intervention is of little value. The real cure has to come from the heart of the addicted; they have to want to change before change can come about. Introducing them to Jesus Christ and praying for them can eventually bring about change, they may never be the same again but at least they have given up the destructive lifestyle they were living. Many do recover this way and become responsible citizens of society.

Jesus Christ is the only true way to recovery from any form of addiction; through Him, all things are possible. He will hold nothing back from those who turn to Him in their times of need. Stand fast in Jesus Christ and He will not disappoint anyone, Jesus can change a life in the wink of an eye and free him or her from what was once a destructive way of life. God promises that all who turn to Him in their times of need and seek forgiveness of their sins shall be blessed with a new life, one acceptable in His sight. As destructive, as an addiction can be there is a way to freedom from that addiction through Jesus Christ and then will one be free at last.

FREE SPIRIT

The condition of the body has nothing to do with the spirit. There are many who have no control over their bodies, they are immobile and completely depend upon others to help them with their daily needs. There mind is not bound by their body, it is a free spirit, free to wander as far as the imagination will allow. As much as these people are prisoners within their own body and may find it difficult to communicate with others they reflect God and His love just as much if not more than most.

Jesus' thinking was so pure that when He looked at the afflicted, He never saw the affliction; He looked beyond it and saw the perfect person. Jesus rebuked the evil spirits and demons on many occasions and delivered many from their afflictions, returning to their homes they rejoiced and praised the Lord for their deliverance. As in the days when Jesus walked among us and healed the sick so does He today. Through prayer and supplication Jesus is available twenty-four seven and can and will heal us of today.

When you see someone who is a prisoner within himself or herself do not look upon them as being anything but what they are, a child of God and as such know that the day will come when they will be free from their affliction, either in this life or the life to come. Be pleasant towards them, encourage them, this will lighten the burden they are carrying and give them courage to face life one day at a time. They have the same ambitions and desires that we all have.

Some of the most brilliant minds are trapped in a handicapped body, but this does not stop them from reflecting Jesus and following the plans he has for their lives. In many ways, they are freer from the limitations of the body than a healthy person is. They concentrate on what they can do and do it well and are not like those who have to do everything. They are also some of the happiest people that you can find. They do not see themselves as being handicapped, but rather see themselves as doing the best they can with what they have. They look beyond their disabilities and see things that most people cannot see. Their minds are not clouded with "I can't", but rather "I will try".

No one has a perfect body; all have handicaps of one kind or another. It is what we do about them that counts, either we overcome them and learn to live with them or we succumb to them and let them ruin our lives. Happiness does not depend upon our physical condition it depends entirely upon our relationship with Jesus Christ and submitting ourselves to His service. True happiness comes from within, not our possessions or our positions in life, the poorest of people are often times happier than those of wealth.

FREEDOM THROUGH
JESUS CHRIST

Thou art truly the son of the living God; Thy "Light" precedeth Thee, it shines in the darkness and the darkness is no more. With Your "Light" cometh healings and man is set free from the bondage of sin. You gave your life upon the cross of Calvary so that all who call upon your name might live a life pleasing to Thee. You defeated Satan while You hung upon that cross and opened the door to eternal life for all who bow before Thee and submit to Your will.

Though we may suffer the afflictions of this world, we will fear them not for You promised us that You will comfort us all the days of our lives and forsake us not. When we leave this life behind You promised eternal life and freedom from our earthly burdens. You demonstrated through Your death, burial, resurrection and ascension that this life is temporal and that there is life beyond the grave and that we may achieve that life through You.

You have stood by me O Lord in my times of need; You have comforted me when I had no place to turn and have sheltered me from the wrath of man. You have healed my body when it was weak and wracked with pain; You lifted me above the chaos that surrounded me and comforted my soul. Your loving hand has guided me through many a trying time and has given me victory over the sins that threatened to engulf me.

As you have promised one day You will return to this earth and this time You will rule with power from on high, all knees shall bow before Thy throne and submit to your will. Woe unto those who reject you, for they shall be cast from Thy sight, never more to enjoy the protection of Your mighty hand. Your followers anxiously await Your return Lord Jesus and look forward to a joyous reunion, never again to be harassed by the temptations of Satan. Truly free to live a life free from the sins that in the past have blinded us.

This world will be transformed before our eyes and we will have nothing but love and praise for You. Your "Light" will shine before all and bring peace to this troubled world. A new beginning for the old will have passed away. What a glorious day that will be, we will weep no more nor suffer from the ills of this world, for all shall be made perfect through Thee. Lord Jesus, You will be our God and we will be your people.

FREEDOM, A GIFT FROM GOD

May freedom ring Lord, may it ring from the mountains to the sea.

May it be heard above the roar of the breaking seas upon the sandy shore.

From north to south, east to west may it ring and be heard above the howling of the wind.

May we stand true to its meaning O Lord, may all men be free, knowing no bounds but Thee.

May we turn not our hearts from Thee O Lord, may we rejoice in Thy love and smell the sweet odor of freedom.

Let its sweet strains be heard by all who follow Thy ways, may it soften the hardest of heats Lord and bring them back to Thee.

May all O Lord sing the songs of freedom, even by me, may these songs fill our hearts with the desire to be a friend to all.

May freedom be a goal for all men to achieve and may it's benefits bless all who seek Thee.

Thank you O Lord for the gift of freedom that is so precious and dear, a gift from you that cannot be taken away by the sword.

Even when imprisoned we can enjoy freedom if only we
follow Thee, true freedom will be enjoyed by all
who seek to live for Thee.

Let freedom ring loud and clear and be held dear by all
who strive to live according to Thee.

Let freedom have no bounds and may it set all men free,
freely you gave it for all to share O Lord, may it
not be held back from those in need.

FROM LIFE TO ETERNAL LIFE

The night of life is far spent; the dawn of a new life is at hand.

Life ebbs and flows, but for the one on the edge of death prays for a safe journey home.

Even those with a great faith have to face death, for death comes to all, great and small.

Only those who are well grounded in the word of God and have accepted Jesus Christ as their Lord and Savior can avoid the second death.

The second death is separation from God for eternity and is reserved for those who live life for themselves without regard for or where they will spend eternity.

Life is a gift from God, not to be taken lightly nor squandered on the material things of life, for they are but for a moment and will rust and decay.

Only the word of God and gifts from above shall survive the rigors of this life, materialism may be pleasurable for the moment, but in no way can materialism survive the muster of God.

Things of this life are meant to make life a little easier, but by no means are they a way to eternal life, in fact they are a hindrance (when put as a priority of life) in ones growth in ones journey towards eternal life.

Few there are who are able to balance both materialism and spiritualism and keep them both in the right perspective, they are both meant to be in balance.

There are those who are so material minded that they are of no heavenly good as well as there are those who are so spiritually minded that they are of no earthly good.

A conflict of thought perhaps, but both materialism and spiritualism are a part of life here on earth and both play an important part in one's life, but as long as God is first and foremost in one's life materialism will be kept in proper perspective.

The way to eternal life is not easy nor was it intended to be, for the trials of life were meant to be a time to reflect on what is the most important in one's life, the struggle to obtain all of the material things of life that one can or a time to reflect on where one wishes to spend eternity.

To put materialism first clouds the road of life and makes materialism a god, to strive for eternal life by putting spiritual things first clears these clouds away and opens one's eyes to the fact that this life is a time to prepare for eternal life.

We go through this life only one time, there are no second chances to change one's mind after death of the flesh as to what is most important in life, materialism or spiritualism, for we either cling to one or the other, the two cannot successfully coexist.

Death separates us from materialism and leaves spiritualism the victor over the materialistic world, as we stand before God we will hear Him declare us fit for His kingdom or deny us the privilege of spending eternity in His presence, then we will fully realize whether our decisions here on earth were to our benefit or our detriment.

GARDEN OF SIN

Oh, how tempting it is to roam through the garden of sin and pick a bouquet that shines so bright and longs to fulfill our every sensual desire. The flower of forbidden love brings to mind that desire of old when we were young and all of those times we played with fire, hoping no one would know.

The times that we sneaked into the movie house to meet the one who made our heart beat with excitement, holding hands and sneaking a kiss or two.

Swimming in the lake late at night under the full of the moon was a time when forbidden love was fulfilled. Though long in the past these memories haunt us and makes us wonder whatever happened to those we once loved and cared for?

The days of old may be gone, but the temptations of the flesh still exist in different ways. Sin never satisfies and is never enough. The more we get the more we want and the more we stray from the way we were raised.

In every stage of life, the temptation to sin is ever present and ever changing. For the unsuspecting the years may change but sin stays the same. Sin is of Satan and his desire is that we leave God out of our lives and succumb to his sadistic ways, resulting in losing our rightful place in the kingdom of God when this world we leave.

With all of the pleasures of sin, we found that our heart was empty and our soul was restless, wanting more than just the pleasures of life. Then came the day that we were lead to dip our finger in the shed blood of Jesus Christ. From that moment on our lives changed and we have never been the same.

Now our days are filled seeking the ways of righteousness. We search the scriptures far into the night, and then sleep the rest of the night away with Jesus on our mind. We awake to a new life, praising God and thanking His Son, Jesus Christ, for giving us a comforter (the Holy Spirit) when He returned to His Father's side.

The Holy Spirit has opened our eyes to many a truth, truths that we have applied to our lives, truths that has taken the desire to roam in the garden of sin away. Like all who have turned their lives over to Jesus Christ, we now spend our hours studying His word and promoting the ways of righteousness whenever we chance to meet someone who was as we were many years ago, lusting in the garden of sin.

GENERATION TO GENERATION

When this life I leave, Lord Jesus, take me by the hand and console me as through the door of death I walk.

Counsel me that I may stand tall and hold my head high as I listen for my name to be called from the book of life.

Blot out my sins and wash me clean in the blood of the Lamb, that my soul may be worthy to spend eternity with Thee.

That I might walk the streets of gold and drink of the water that flows from Thy throne, and eat of the fruit of the tree of life.

Grant peace to the generations that are yet to come, guide them as You have guided me.

Speak to their hearts as they struggle to do Thy will in their lives.

Open the door so that Thy light may be as a beacon of hope unto their souls and light unto their path.

As their time comes to leave this earth grant them the same privilege that You have granted me, the privilege of spending eternity with Thee.

Grant O Lord from generation to generation that Thy love shall shine through the clouds of sin and be as a lighthouse with it's light searching in the dark of night for all who are lost in the sea of sin.

May Your love, Your peace, Your comfort and forgiveness be to all generations until the return of Your Son, Jesus Christ.

These things we ask in His Holy Name, Amen.

GOD CAN SAVE

God loves the sinner and can set them free, but only if they agree, for even God cannot save a sinner without their consent.

God created man in His own image and set him free to live life as he pleases, otherwise man would be like a puppet on a string, dancing to a tune over which he has no control.

In this world sin abounds, tempting man to take his eyes off of God and do the will of Satan rather than God.

In the final days the sheep will be separated from the goats; the sheep have a shepherd to follow and they know their shepherds voice, whereas the goats go their own way disregarding the voice of the shepherd.

Man is the same, man will either follow God or he will follow Satan, depending upon what he wants out of life, those who seek earthly treasures will ignore the calling of God on their life whereas those who choose spiritual gratification over earthly treasures will live by and obey the commands of God.

Many there are who start out in life living life their way and find that that lifestyle is actually leading them down the wrong path, for they find no real satisfaction in the way that they are living, something is missing and they do not know quite what it is.

Over time they realize that they are discontent with living life their way and begin a search for a better way of life, either through friends or other sources they look around and see people who are content in whatever situation they may find themselves.

This in turn can stir within one the desire to have the same contentment, then one day it dawns upon them that it is God who they have been searching for all of the time and finally declare that they too want what God has to offer.

All conversions are different in one way or the other, but the results are the same, a soul saved from the ravages of Satan, some conversions are instantaneous while others are more gradual and even others seem to have been from youth through the influence of family and or friends.

Regardless of how we come to Christ we all come for the same reason, within our soul is a desire to serve God and through service obtain eternal life, through service includes the acceptance of God's Son, Jesus Christ, as our personal Lord and Savior and through the acceptance of Jesus as the Son of God we obtain eternal life.

It is not always clear at first but the longer we stay true to our conviction that Jesus holds the key to eternity the sooner we give our lives over to Him and serve him in whatever capacity He wills for our lives, through service for the kingdom of God we leave earthly desires behind and find the contentment that we saw in others before we turned our lives over to God.

All have to make the decision to serve God and be saved or to serve our own selfish desires to please the flesh, the two are contrary one to the other, by doing nothing we have already chosen to please the flesh and face eternity separated from God, to choose to serve God we assure our place with God for eternity.

Yes, God can save a sinner, but it your choice and my choice to accept His offer or not, you and I do control what influence we allow God to have on our lives, I have accepted God's offer, have you?

GOD IS ALL IN ALL

Before the great flood, humankind worshiped gods of their choice and ignored the one and true God. God grieved that He had created man and was going to destroy all of His created beings. A man by the name of Noah found favor in the eyes of God and God instructed Noah and his three sons (Ham, Shem and Japheth) to build an Ark. When it was finished, he was to gather two of every species (male and female) and put them into the Ark, for God was going to cause it to rain for forty days and forty nights to destroy all living things upon the face of the earth. Noah was obedient to the word of God and Noah was six hundred years of age when the waters receded from the face of the earth. Through obedience to the word of God Noah and his family were the only survivors of the great flood. They went forth and repopulated the earth, so we of today are descendents of Noah.

Those who scorned Noah as he built the Ark refused to change their ways. They scoffed Noah and his sons and when the rains came, they were refused refuge within the Ark and thus all of mankind and the remaining beasts of the earth were destroyed because of their refusal to listen to and obey God. God showed His absolute control and authority over all of the earth and all who lived on the earth, including all of the creatures of the earth. After the flood, God made a covenant with Noah and sealed that covenant by placing a bow in the clouds.

When observing a rainbow today remember that, it represents God's promise to never destroy man from the face of the earth again by the use of water.

Our modern ways of life are not that much different from the days of Noah. Many today still worship pagan gods and are following in the footprints of their ancient ancestors. There are many idolaters today and if they had their way, they would eliminate all semblance of Christianity and worship Satan. They live by the code that if it feels right do it, they even advocate that when one reaches a certain age then they should be euthanized, thus relieving society of having to take care of them. As Christians, we know that this is Satanic in nature and Satan's way of achieving his goal of destroying all of God's creation and created beings that he can.

There comes a time in the lives of all that they have to make the decision as to who they are going to follow and worship, God or Satan. We come to that fork in the road where on one hand we can choose to walk the straight and narrow path that leads to eternal life or go along with the crowd and walk the wide road with all of its temptations and earthly riches. This is a personal decision and each individual has to make that choice for him or herself and by themselves. The narrow road is lined with guardrails made of the laws of God and serve as laws by which one conducts the affairs of their life. Whereas the wide road of life has no guardrails or boundaries or rules to live by, many there be who fall into this category and before they realize it they find themselves spending eternity in the fires of hell. The followers of our triune God find themselves enjoying the treasures of heaven.

Each individual is in complete control of how they live their lives, thus in control of where they will spend eternity. From Genesis to Revelation we witness the struggle of all time, the struggle of good and evil, we are in a spiritual battle that Satan is waging against God and all who choose to follow Him. You and I have the privilege of reading the book of Revelation and know the outcome of this battle between good and evil. God always has and always will be triumphant over all manner of evil and He extends that victory to all who forsake their evil ways through repentance and come to Him and commit their lives to His service. Spiritual death is separation from God for eternity (hell); eternal life is spending eternity in God's presence (heaven). Deny God and die, follow God and live, it is just that simple.

GOD IS CALLING

Take time out of your busy schedule, put self aside, follow the teachings of Jesus Christ, and see the difference it will make in your life. Your attitude towards others will change in the process.

To live by the dictates of the Holy Scriptures will not only enhance our own lives, it will influence what other people think about you and encourage them to make the necessary changes in their own lives.

Living with the Holy Scriptures as our guide will change us both spiritually and morally and help us to see others in the same "Light" as we want them to see us.

Glorifying God in all aspects of our lives will bring people and nations together and eliminate conflicts between nations, restore peace and enable us to use the resources to wage war to eliminate poverty and hunger throughout the world.

It is a spiritual battle that we are engaged in, conform to the will of God and sin can be overcome. The main ingredient in our struggle against sin is prayer, a prayer that we ourselves can change and see others as children of God and thus as equals.

To love one another, as we want to be loved can change enemies into friends and as friends, we can change the whole world. As Jesus showed His love for us by being a sacrifice for the sins of the whole world upon the cross of Calvary so should we reflect that same love in dealings with our fellowman.

Stand and be counted among those who are willing to sacrifice all for the glory of God, step forth in faith and let it be known that your love and devotion to God comes before anything else in your life.

It takes courage and the conviction that you can make a difference in the lives of others through Jesus Christ; shy not away from that which you have been called to do.

All are called by God to step forward and do their part in this sin-filled world, called to light a "Light" and let it shine in the lives of others and encourage them to follow the dictates of the Holy Scriptures, enabling them to achieve eternal life.

There is no greater pleasure and satisfaction in knowing that you are fulfilling what you have been called by God to do. Do not glorify yourself or your deeds, but humbly give all credit and glory to God.

All together, we can accomplish much; each one doing their part can change the world into a better place to live and bring about peace where there was once discord and strife.

Satan is a powerful force in this world, he is a liar and the father of all lies and will do his best to keep us from doing our part in bringing about peace among the peoples of the world.

Satan's objective is to keep as many as he can from becoming a follower of Jesus Christ. However, Satan is under the control of God and God will only allow him to tempt anyone to follow him; Satan cannot force anyone to submit to his will.

Everyone wants to be a winner, so it behooves all to submit themselves to the will of God and do their part in spreading His word to the whole world. As foretold in the Holy Scriptures, in the end Satan, his fallen angels and all who submit to the will of Satan will be cast into the Lake of Fire, leaving the world a place of eternal peace under the auspices of our Lord and Savior, Jesus Christ.

GOD IS SUPREME

John 1:1 In the beginning was the word, and the word was with God, and the word was God.

Thus, God through His Son, Jesus Christ, created everything, He created heaven and all things therein, created He the earth and all things therein is, and declared all things to be good. He set the universe in motion and was satisfied with His creation.

God created man from the dust of the ground, breathed the breath of life into him, and made him a living soul. Male and female created He them. He placed them in the Garden of Eden and gave them dominion over it. This worked well until the day that the serpent beguiled Eve and tempted her to eat of the forbidden fruit of the tree of knowledge of good and evil and in turn, Eve enticed Adam to eat of the same fruit. They both became aware of their nakedness and hid from the presence of God.

Up until now, man did not have to provide for himself, for God provided his every need, but after disobedience God ban them both from the Garden of Eden, to live apart from God's presence. Then Adam had to provide his own needs, through his own efforts. From then to the present time man has had to provide for himself.

As time passed, man multiplied and so did sin. Satan was out to seek revenge for being cast out of heaven, because of his disobedience by wanting to be equal with God. Man became so corrupt that God was going to destroy His created beings from the face of the earth, but Noah found favor with God and Noah and his three sons and their wives built an ark and through God's instructions, they gathered two of every species into the ark. Then God released the waters of the earth and all other living beings along with all creatures were destroyed by the flood.

At this time God made a covenant with man that, He (God) would never again destroy man from the face of the earth. As a sign of His covenant God placed, a rainbow in the sky and that rainbow would remind man of God's covenant. Man once again populated the earth and once again, Satan spread his sinful ways.

All during this period God kept an avenue open whereby there would be an unbroken line of ancestry by which He could send his Son, Jesus Christ into the world, that through him the world might be saved. Jesus came as a newborn babe through a virgin birth and lived among His created beings. He spread His Father's word among the people of the earth as a guide as to how they should live their lives. Jesus demonstrated that sin can and could be overcome through adherence to the word of God. Jesus took the sins of man upon Himself and allowed Himself to be crucified on the cross of Calvary for the sins of the whole world. Through His death, burial, and resurrection Jesus overcame the sins of the world and set man free from the bondage of sin. By doing so, Jesus defeated Satan at his own game and opened the door to eternal life to all who would bear His name and follow Him. Satan is a defeated adversary, going around like a roaring lion trying to devour all who stray and fall into sin. Jesus has the power to forgive sin and asks all to come to Him seeking forgiveness of their sins and through Him be born again.

This ultimate act of love on the part of God is His final attempt to get man to change his ways and return to Him while there is still time, for the day fast approaches when it will be too late to change. True to His word, God has not interfered with man's choice as to whom he will follow, God or Satan and God will honor whichever choice man makes. To follow God is to inherit eternal life; to follow Satan is to inherit eternal damnation.

Satan knows that his final destination is the lake of fire, where the worm never dies, commonly known as hell. Before this happens, he will entice as many of God's people that he can to follow him. He can in no way force anyone to follow him, his only power is the power of temptation. Satan only has the power that God allows him to have. God is supreme and in the end, God shall prevail. Let there be no doubt about that.

GOD WILL SUPPLY

No matter what the temptation might be God will provide a way to resist that temptation, thus enabling you to be true to your calling.

All who seek to do the will of God in their lives will take all things to God in prayer and wait upon Him to guide them in the way that He has for them to follow.

Those who succumb to the temptations of Satan will suffer the consequences of disobedience either here or hereafter. However, if that person goes before the throne of God and confesses that transgression God will forgive them of that sin and restore peace within them.

Proof of repentance of sin is a changed life, both in how they live and act towards their fellowman, not just temporarily, but for the rest of their life.

In Romans 3:23, "For all have sinned and come short of the glory of God." KJV No one is exempt from sinning; it is what we do and how we handle the temptation to sin that determines our future.

God leaves such decisions up to each person as to whether they fall victim to the sadistic ways of Satan or the putting on the complete armor of God in their struggle against the temptations of Satan, thus turning their life over to God rather than Satan.

As the old saying goes, "There is a silver lining to every dark cloud." Seek God and His righteousness and He will provide a solution to all dark clouds in your life, thus representing that silver lining.

It is all too easy to succumb to the temptations of Satan, for he can make wrong seem right. Once exposed to the truths of God as found in the Holy Scriptures sin will be exposed as being wrong no matter how much creature comfort that sin might provide.

Sin is sin no matter what form it might take, it is up to you and up to me to decide whether to follow God or act on the temptations that bombard us every day. Sin is the act of submitting to what might seem right at the moment and doing nothing about it when you realize that it is wrong.

God is a loving God and will forgive a repentant heart and welcome them back into His sheepfold and provide a righteous path for them to follow. The pathway to eternal life is straight and narrow whereas the pathway to destruction is wide and full of temptations that pleases the flesh.

GOD'S GLORY

Peace will come to all who follow the Lord.

The unrepentant sinners will perish by their own hand,

The righteous shall dwell in the presence of the Lord forever.

Jesus will lead the righteous to the waters of life.

Jesus came to free the righteous from the ravages of sin.

Every living soul will witness the second coming of Jesus Christ.

On that day, this world will be changed forever and never more will Satan be the Prince of this world.

Jesus died for the sins of the whole world and gave hope for the destitute.

Peace belongs to those who stand in the shadow of the Almighty.

Give all glory, honor and praise to God.

GOING HOME

I have walked the ocean's edge, I have climb the mountains high, the desert sun has set upon my tired head, no matter where I have wandered the Lord has lead me all of the way.

His love has kept me safe from all harm and His Son, Jesus Christ, has walked with me every step of the way. He has guided my footsteps through rain and sunshine, never once has He let me walk alone, His guiding hand has gone on before me and paved the way.

When I thought that, I could go no further He revealed His love to me. The trials He had for me to endure lost their fearsome threat and endure them I have. Not by my own shrewdness have I survived, but only by the grace of God, I have endured.

When entering the unknown, I feared to tread, but Jesus went before me and I followed His "Light" to higher ground. There I stood in amazement as I surveyed the work of His creative hand.

From early childhood to age of old, I have learned to turn to Jesus when things go wrong, He has opened the doors that He wanted me to pass through. Never once did I have to journey alone.

Walking through the trials of life, I have feared not for Jesus has gone before me and smoothed the way. At times, the way has been blocked by the temptations of Satan, but the "Light" of Jesus has guided me and saved me from his evil hand.

The waves of darkness has pounded upon my life's shore, but the love of God has kept me from being swept out to sea, The sunlight of His love has been a saving grace and I now walk with my head high and my eyes upon His throne, for no other way could I have survived.

It is by the grace of God that I have lived a life that reveals that all who turn to Him in good times and bad will one day hear Him say, "Come my child, it is time to come home. Fear not the journey for my Son, Jesus Christ, has paved the way."

"I sent Him to earth to take your sins upon Him and free you from the fowler's hand. By the way of the cross He paid the price of your sins and drove the darkness away. Turn to Jesus and He will walk with you and take you unto Himself when from the earth you leave."

With advice like this fear not what you encounter on your life's journey, for Jesus has walked before you and smoothed out the bumps that you have and will encounter along the way.

Praise Him and open your heart to Jesus and no one can keep you from fulfilling what God has for you to do. Through prayer and supplication fulfill your calling and when you leave this life behind you will hear Jesus calling your name and saying, "Fear not. Take my hand, for it is time to come home."

GUIDE ME LORD IN THE PATHS THAT YOU WANT ME TO TROD

Guide me Lord Jesus, lead me to the path
that I should trod.

Hold my hand and keep me from stumbling,
keep me from wandering or falling asleep.

I have not found a job that You cannot do,
Your love is all I seek.

The paths of this life wander far and wide,
but none is as great as the one
that leads to You.

You have held my hand when I have
stumbled, You have filled my heart
with joy when I have been sad.

I see Your face before me and feel the
warmth of Your love.

Onward and upward we all must go,
till the day we stand at Thy feet,
seeking Your will and praying
that we will be worthy of
Your love.

Through darkness I have wandered,
a glimpse of Your "Light" has
kept me full of hope that
one day I might reside
with you.

Bless all of Your children as You
have blessed me, for all are
Your children. From the
cradle to the grave all
belong to Thee.

Thank You O Lord for the love
that You have shown towards
a sinner like me.

HE IS CALLING

Come all who wish to live, come; take a trip with me,
read your Bible, every word and live accordingly,
then we will be on our way.

Wait not for someone else to lead the way, step forward
and be among those who believe.

Listen for the voice of our great Shepherd, it will be soft
and yet heard the world around upon the
winds of time.

His outstretched hands will welcome all who bend their
knee, He will heal them all.

His eyes will reflect His Father's love, seeing beyond our
sinful ways He gave His life for you and me.

He is calling for sinners to repent, never demanding
though He is in command.

Jesus came to serve and be as a doorway to life beyond
the grave, it is for all who choose to walk through.

One by one we will leave this life behind, for those who
believe there will be no fear, for the great Shepherd
is waiting on the other side.

HE SHALL RETURN TRIUMPHANT

The mighty shall fall under the weight of the Lord
and the humble shall be exalted by the
power of the Almighty.

No one shall stay the same, all shall be changed.
The Lord is able to build up or to tear
down according to His will.

No two people are created the same, for the Lord
has many places to fill.

The closed mind shall be opened and the weak in
spirit shall be made strong through the
word of God.

The eye of the evil one shall be plucked out, the blind
shall see, the Lord shall endureth forever.

He cometh, we know not when, when He does come
we know that all things shall become new.

The old shall be cast aside and the new shall triumph
and stand for all of eternity.

The weak of heart shall faint, but His mighty hand
shall restore.

All shall become as one and be cleansed in the blood
of the Lamb.

All eyes shall see him as he is and nevermore roam.

Sin shall be plucked from their hearts and nevermore rule the day.

Darkness shall fade away, the "Light" of the Lord shall take its place.

Man shall cast his earthly treasures aside and fill his heart with the word of the Lord.

All shall sweep their closets clean and pray to the Lord with gratitude.

The tide of iniquity shall rise no more, it will be replaced with the path that leads to everlasting life.

From the highest to the lowest, all shall bend their knees before the throne of God, all tongues shall confess their sins.

The fires of hell shall be fueled by the tares as they are separated from the wheat at time of harvest.

The wicked heart shall no longer beat, it shall be replaced by the love of the Lord.

As the end draws neigh all eyes shall be opened to witness the coming of the Lord and the end of time.

Fear shall rule those who do not love the Lord, but the humble of heart shall rise triumphantly and meet Him on High.

In the twinkling of an eye all shall change, never again to be the same.

The earth shall pass from under our feet, the sun, and moon and the stars shall fade away.

The "Light" of life shall shine upon our hearts and guide us on our way.

We will sin no more and our eyes shall see the glory of the Lord.

The righteous shall triumph and the wicked will reap their just rewards and be no more.

True love shall rule the day and the night as the old passes away.

The righteous shall hunger no more, the streets paved with gold shall feel soft under their feet.

The waters of the river of life shall quench their thirst and cool their brow.

The reign of sin shall forever be gone, all of the righteous shall praise almighty God, never more to wander from His ways.

HE TOUCHED ME

Yes, Jesus loves me and He touched me and I will never be the same.

Jesus changed my life in the wink of an eye, for Jesus touched me and made me whole.

His "Light" did shine so bright the night He touched me and changed my life.

His "Light" drove the darkness of sin away, my eyes saw the beauty of His countenance and I felt His love as never before.

Though temptations still abound I now have a fortress to protect me, it is the "Light" of my Savior that even Satan must obey.

Were it not for the "Light" of Jesus surely my ship of life would be lost forever in the sea of sin where the sea billows of sin roll upon my shore of life.

Yes, Jesus touched me just before I was lost in the sea of sin, never to hear my Master's voice again.

Oh, how different things are since I saw the "Light" that set me free, I now have the desire to do His will and glorify His name.

I talk about Him and write about Him to let people know that Jesus still lives and loves them and wants to make them whole as He did me the night He touched me.

Praise Him and adore Him, for He holds the power of the universe in His hands and will save all who forsake their wicked ways and follow Him.

It is better to change ones ways and turn to the "Light" of Jesus and live by His word than it is to live life for one's self and end up separated from God, Jesus, and the Holy Spirit for eternity.

Jesus holds the key to eternal life and only through Him can we come unto the Father and become a child of the King.

Jesus can touch you just as He touched me, turn to Him and let Him change your life forever and set you free.

HEALING POWWER OF GOD

Healing of the heart, mind and soul comes from God; He offers man relief from his daily burdens by the laying down of those burdens before His throne through the power of prayer.

Through his love for mankind God sent his one and only Son, Jesus Christ, into this sin filled world to turn on the healing "Light" and offer man an alternative way of life than what the Prince of this world offers, those who take advantage of God's offer of a new way of life find that they too can live in this sin filled world without letting sin overwhelm them.

We all are in one way or another affected by the sin that prevails around us but we need not be caught up in sin and lose our way in this world for we have a helper by the name of the Holy Spirit whom Jesus sent when He ascended into heaven to take His place by His Father's side after His death, burial and resurrection.

Jesus Christ did not have to come to earth and take our place on the cross of Calvary, He came out of love and obedience to His Father's will, He paid in full the price of sin as He shed His blood while on the cross.

Jesus paid the price of sin for the whole world, even those who today are killing their neighbor because they do not bow down and worship the same god as they do, if these terrorist would only turn to Jesus, He in turn would forgive them of their deadly sins and restore them to their rightful place, thus healing them as He has healed all who accept Him as their Lord and Savior.

Jesus Christ cannot heal anyone without their consent, when God created man he gave man a free will and even God cannot go against the free will of man without man's permission, it is also true that when man dies he will stand before God and make an accounting of how he lived his life here on earth and if he did or did not accept Jesus Christ as his Lord and Savior, for it is only through accepting Jesus Christ as our Lord and Savior that we can spend eternity in the presence of God.

After passing through the door of death it is too late to change and receive mercy from God for the way that we lived our lives here on earth, this is a time of separating the tares from the wheat, a time when the tares will be cast into the fires of hell and the wheat gathered into God's storehouse, there will wailing and gnashing of teeth.

All of mankind has or will have an opportunity before they pass from this life to adhere to the will of God and become a disciple of Jesus Christ so that on the Day of Judgment they will not have any excuse for not doing so, through the healing power of God all things are possible.

Submitting oneself to the will of God brings a peace beyond understanding; it can heal the body, mind and soul and make them wholly acceptable in the eyes of God, this is what this life should be all about, a time to allow the healing powers of God to work in our lives and create in us a new being.

God loves every man, woman, and child on the face of this Earth and He wants everyone to spend eternity with Him, but due to the sin that came into this world through disobedience to God's will there will be a Day of Judgment, but through the healing power of God man can avoid the consequences of his disobedience.

God will accept all who forsake their sinful ways and accept His Son, Jesus Christ as their personal Savior, have you made that decision, now is the day and hour to do so, come before the throne of God and make your commitment to Him, this is a personal thing and only you can do it. It matters not what station of life you are in, God is calling, have you heeded that call?

HEAVEN OR HELL

Death is but a doorway to a new life. Listening to those who have had what is called a near death experience one can get a glimpse of what is yet to come. Such an experience can and does change ones outlook on life. It can also change the way in which one lives. Those who have accepted Jesus Christ as their Lord and Savior need to have no fear of death. When one-steps through the door of death, they are completely free from the devious way of Satan, for Satan has no jurisdiction in heaven and they will be free to soar with the angels.

Anyone who chooses to follow a path contrary to God will face an afterlife that we refer to as hell. Those who have not lived a godly life and have had a near death experience paint a different picture of what they have witnessed. They come back telling of the dreadful and horrible sights that they have seen and most have given up their evil ways and sought the love and protection of God. Those who refuse to give up their evil ways for whatever reason shall be separated from God for eternity when they pass through the door of death. Their lust for evil and the power, and money was so great that nothing could deter them from it, in the false belief that they are beyond saving. Nothing could be further from the truth, for Jesus Christ will forgive any and all who forsake their evil ways and ask Him for forgiveness of their sins. Christ will embrace all who seek Him and spare them the torments of hell.

In no way will our loving Triune God impose their will upon anyone. It has to be a free choice on the part of man in seeking God's love and forgiveness. All have sinned and fallen short of the glory of God, but being the loving God that He is He will embrace all who step out in faith and seek His will and welcome them back to His sheepfold, completely cleansed from all unrighteousness. Jesus is not willing that even one be lost, but He leaves that decision completely up to the individual. There is no love greater than the love of our Triune God, God the Father, God the Son and God the Holy Spirit.

All, at one time or another have to make the decision where they want to spend eternity, with God or with Satan. Those who put off making that decision are as much as saying, "I am young and have a lifetime ahead of me to decide where I want to spend eternity. For now I have all I need, I will worry about that later." The truth is later may never come, for no one knows the day of their demise, only God knows that day. Others may influence our decision-making, but it is up to each one to make the final decision. Once we take our final breath here on earth it is too late for decision-making, God gives us up to that moment to decide who we want to spend eternity with, but after that, it is too late, God Himself makes the decision for us.

Everyone in one way or another have some fear of dying, some more than others. It is an experience that all will have to go through, the only exception will be those who are living the day that Jesus returns to Earth and they will be caught up in the heaven with Him. With a good background in the ways of God and knowledge of the Holy Scriptures one can overcome their fear of death and look upon death as an opportunity to spend eternity with God. A good friend who was dying from cancer said just before her death, "It is time to go home." What a wonderful way to look at death. Instead of fearing death, she embraced death without fear of any kind for she had a great love for God and knew in her heart that God was sustaining her in her time of need. Everyone can have that same experience if they will embrace God now while they still have the chance.

All must remember that as children of God, they do not have any control of when they will leave this life behind, but they do have control over where they will spend eternity. Our future is but a tick of the clock of life away, no one is promised tomorrow, but we do have the promise that if we accept Jesus Christ as our Lord and Savior and believe that He is the Son of God then we will inherit eternal life. All are children of God and as such have the choice of spending eternity in heaven or hell.

HELP ME ALONG THE WAY

Let the stars shine this night and
guide me along the way.

Let the moon brighten my path so
that I will not stray.

Let the ocean's roar fill my ears
as a song from Thee.

Let my feet roam no more, that I
may stand before Thee.

Steer my ship of life, and keep it from
floundering on the rocks of sin.

When the winds of sin blow and try to flood my
soul, may your mighty hand hold it a bay.

The morning dew will quench my thirst as
through the deserts of life, I roam.

Let not my feet stumble as age
takes my youth away.

May the sun warm my face before
my body grows cold.

May I stand before Thee O Lord and
praise thy mighty name.

For yours I am Lord, tell
me what to say.

Let not my mouth be closed when it comes to you
O Lord, let it shout from the rooftops so that
all may hear that which you have to say.

HELPING HAND

Many of the problems we face on a daily basis can be overwhelming and after a prolonged period, some will solve their problems by taking their own lives. This unfortunately is the wrong approach to putting lives problems in their proper perspective. The Bible says that man will have problems and trials all the days of his life, but when handled in the right way problems are meant to draw us close to our Creator, God. He wants us to bring all of our trials and problems to Him and in His infinite wisdom He will guide us through our trying times and help us resolve our problems in an amicable way.

Those who choose to take their own lives because of overwhelming circumstances many times do so because they do not have anyone to turn to for help and understanding. They feel alone and abandoned with no or very little faith to fall back on. It is in times like these that can be an opportunity to grow in faith and trust in God. As learned from the scriptures, God will not put any more burdens upon us that we are not capable of handling. True, some illnesses or tragic circumstances can be overwhelming and seemingly have no answer, but when taken before the throne of God through prayer and total reliance upon Him will result in either healing or comfort and peace of mind even unto death.

Since the introduction of sin in man's life, it has been a constant struggle between good and evil.

Sin manifests itself in many different ways, one may have physical problems, another may have mental problems, others may have sociological problems, but they all come from the same source, Satan. All bad thoughts, bad actions, bad relationships and anything that is not of God come from Satan. Satan is the Prince of this world and as such, he has the authority to tempt us to turn from God and follow him. Satan only has the power of temptations and cannot force anyone to do anything against his or her will. This was decreed by God and revealed in the book of Job in the Old Testament. In both chapter 1 verse 12 and in chapter 2 verse 6 God gives Satan permission to do whatever he wants to Job, but he could not take his life.

When one door closes, God will open another, in this way God will if we allow Him guide us through our life and life's trials. God will not abandon us, even though it may seem that way when we are going through the hard times of life. He is always there to help, it is our choice whether to call upon His help when in need or try to work out our own problems without His help. God will never force His will upon anyone without that person's permission. In many cases this is where our pride gets in the way, we say we do not need any help; we can handle the problem on our own, when in fact with this kind of attitude we make our problems worse. Many have succumbed to the temptations of Satan because they allowed pride to get in the way. Instead of pride, go before the throne of God with a humble heart and seek His help. Being humble does not mean we are weak, it means that we recognize that God knows us better than we know ourselves and that He is the one who can guide us through our difficult times the way that is best for us.

God is ready, willing and able to help any and all who call upon His name, He will turn no one away, nor will he put preconditions on His help or His love. God loved us enough to send His one and only Son, Jesus Christ into this sin-filled world to be a sacrifice for the sins of the whole world, so that all who believe on Him might be saved. God's helping hand is available any time of day or night and His timing is always perfect. Wrestle not alone with the trials and tribulations of this world, turn to God and He will guide you and help you in ways you never even thought of.

HIS WORLD

The stars by night, the sun by day reveals the beauty of God's creation, this world He created just for you and me.

From seed the trees grow straight and tall and declare the majesty of God, they are for the benefit of man.

When in full bloom the flowers fill the air with their fragrant smell, pleasing to all who pass by and pause in a moment of silent prayer to the one who came and fulfilled His Father's will.

For this is God's world, given to man to till the soil and reap the harvest of his toil, from God to man it came and one day return it will.

Man is just a sojourner on this star among stars, it is up to him to care for his home away from home and leave it one day he will.

God has had His hand on this planet called Earth from the beginning of time and keep it He will, for His love for man will never die.

In fact, God sent His one and only Son, Jesus Christ, unto Earth to save man from the clutches of the evil one.

Jesus shed His blood on the cross of Calvary and washed us white as snow, making us worthy to spend eternity in the presence of our creator, blessed be He who did this for you and for me.

When Jesus returned to His heavenly home He created a place in heaven for all who believe, one day He will return to earth and take His faithful followers to their new home, one that now we cannot see.

Therefore, as you journey throughout this world drink in the beauty that our creator has created and praise His Holy Name, for it is only through His love that we are here.

Remember this is our Father's world, care for it as if it were your own, prepare for the day that Jesus will return and be sure to include a "Thank you Jesus for all that You have done for sinners like me."

HOPE

All Christians live in the hope of eternal life through our Lord and Savior, Jesus Christ. On the cross of Calvary Jesus took your sins and mine upon himself and shed His blood so that we can be free from the bondage of sin, the price of which is eternal death. The hope of eternal life burns bright and is worth more than all the riches that this world has to offer. The riches of this world will one-day decay, but eternal life is for eternity. Eternal life cannot be bought at any price nor can it be sold, it is a gift from God, free to all who declare that Jesus Christ is the Son of God.

H—How is your relationship with Jesus Christ? Do you know that you know that if you died today that you would spend eternity with Jesus Christ? If in doubt then accept Jesus, as your Lord and Savior now, today for tomorrow may be too late.

O—Open your heart to Jesus Christ and receive the blessings that He has for you. Jesus is the giver of all good gifts, freedom from the bondage of sin, contentment in whatever situation you might find yourself, peace beyond understanding, most of all a love that has no end or equal.

P—Prepare yourself for eternal life now; God has allotted each one so many days to live and only He knows when our days will end. Read the

Bible and apply the teachings to your life, be as a "Light" set upon a hill. Let your light so shine before men that it will encourage them to follow your example.

E—Every day awaken with a renewed heart and be a blessing to your fellow man. Pray for those who need prayer. Give of yourself and ask nothing in return. God loves a cheerful giver and will bless them who give in His name. Seek to do the will of God in your life receive the hope of eternal life.

HOW DO YOU LIVE

What fools we mortal be, we chase the wind and yet we never find tranquility or peace of mind. Our soul is never at rest. From pillar to post we wander in pursuit of what we think will fulfill our every want.

We call it trying to find ourselves and yet we never think to look within, for how can something so simple bring the peace that we are looking for?

I will just work a little harder and the extra change will surly buy me something that will satisfy my inner longings, thus I will find peace of mind and my soul will be content.

We often marry in hopes of finding love, something to fulfill that which we have dreamed of as a child and we find ourselves burdened with cares we never thought would be ours to bear.

Driving a fancy car, dinning on fine food and wines may fulfill our desires, but deep within, our soul cries for peace.

We look in all the wrong places and find that wealth, prestige and fame are just another word for failure in our pursuit of what we thought would bring us peace and contentment.

Then one day we meet someone who is clothed in our old cast offs and yet find that they are happy and never fret about tomorrow, their eyes shine with contentment, not sorrow.

They live in what we would call poverty and yet they seem to have no problems and are content in the circumstances that they find themselves. How can this be? They have nothing, I have everything anyone could want and yet I am not half as happy as they appear to be.

One Sunday you happen to see this person grace the church that you have never entered, for in your way of thinking church is for those who cannot think for themselves and need someone to tell them how to live.

Then one day you find yourself down and out, your wealth and high living had gone down the drain when Wall Street went bust. Through tears and disgrace, you search far and near for your daily needs.

Then one Sunday morning as you were passing by an open church door you heard those inside singing praises to the Lord on high. Your heart was troubled as you hurried by; two blocks away you stopped and could still hear the singing of that hymn and felt the urge to join them.

Slowly you turned around and made your way to that church door. There you hesitated before entering, wondering what people would think if you entered therein. Your fears were quelled as someone took you by the hand and said, "Welcome, please join us?"

With a sheepish smile, you made your way to a vacant seat in the back pew. Still tense you opened the hymnal and joined in singing praises to the Lord. After the sermon, the preacher asked all who wanted, to come and kneel at the altar for special prayer.

Your first instinct was to get up and leave, but for some reason you could not. With your heart, racing you felt drawn to the altar; slowly you made your way forward, and fell to your knees at the altar rail. With eyes closed, not knowing quite what to pray about you felt the preachers hand on your shoulder and heard him say, "How may I serve you today/"

With that, tears began to flow down your cheek as you told him your burdens and at that moment, you felt as though a great weight had been lifted from your shoulders. For the first time in your life, you felt the love you had pursued for so many years.

You had allowed God to enter your life and when you did, it mattered not that your wealth and way of life was no more, for you had found the peace and love you had so desperately pursued. At that moment, your life was changed forever.

That Sunday when you left that church you knew without a doubt that you had been on a journey from darkness to "Light" and you had found the peace and love that had eluded you when you lived the life of the wealthy with disregard for your spiritual being.

New doors were opened to you and soon you were back on your feet, living the life, that God had planned for you and you realized that your new lifestyle was worth more than all of the enticements that your old lifestyle had to offer.

You now reached out to others not as fortunate as yourself; each time God's love filled your heart to overflowing. Then with the realization that earthly wealth and prestige is as dust in the wind, here today and gone tomorrow and that God is the supplier of all of our needs.

HOW HAVE YOU CHANGED

Do you claim to be a Christian, if so how has being a Christian changed your life, have you given up your old habits in favor of new ones, do you intend to or have you committed the rest of your life to the service of God, have you accepted your neighbor (whether he lives next door or on the other side of the world) as an equal in the eyes of God?

These and other questions have to be answered in order to show that your life has been changed and that you are serious about your commitment to a Christian way of life, they have to be more than answered, one must live a life exemplary of their beliefs and by doing so others may see God through them.

At first this is not an easy way to go or to live, for in many cases it requires one to give up a lucrative business, a change of residence, leaving old friends behind and making new friends, friends who are living a Christian life, embracing a complete new way of life and lifestyle.

These are trying times, to change is not easy for the old style of living keeps beckoning you to return and take up your old habits again, but as time passes your new way of living becomes more comfortable and slowly the urge to go back to your old lifestyle fades and you begin to look forward to the changes that have yet to be made.

God does require that the seeking heart walk a straight and narrow path, one that at first seems to be too much to ask of anyone, it is a path that one has to become comfortable with, and has to overcome the sneers and jeers of the un-believing world.

A Christian often times may be required to put their life on the line in the defense of the kingdom of God, putting God before life itself is no easy decision to make and yet it is far better to stand up for Christianity and lose your life than it is to give in to the dictates of some evil force and become a victim of Satan' sadistic ways.

To lose one's life in defense of a Christian way of life is to gain eternal life, to do otherwise is putting oneself in danger of the judgment of God, we cannot serve two masters, we cannot serve God and the ways of the world at the same time, one has to choose one or the other, far too many choose the wrong path thinking they are doing right.

Satan is very deceptive in making one think that God is not serious about keeping oneself in tune with his ways, that is why all things must be tried against the Scriptures to see if they are of God or of Satan, if of Satan the Scriptures will reveal the flaw or flaws and guide one away from them, if of God, then the Scriptures will encourage one to follow them.

Change and the desire to change does not come easy at first, but the more one looks to the future and takes seriously that there is life beyond the grave and that now is the time to prepare for that life the easier it becomes to make the necessary changes in one's lifestyle to conform to what God wants for them, mainly, to spend eternity with Him, to do otherwise is opening oneself to the judgment of God and this will not be a very pleasant position to put oneself in.

God made all the arraignments necessary for change through His Son, Jesus Christ, for God sent him to earth to be a sacrifice for the sins of the whole world and that through Him all may come to repentance and receive eternal life, for there is no other way in which you and I can come to God and receive our heavenly reward of spending eternity in His presence.

With change from a rebellious lifestyle to an obedient lifestyle comes true happiness and true contentment, for when we commit our lives to the service of our triune God we will be guided in the way that we should live and the doors will be opened to get us where we should be, it is through obedience to the ways of God the Father, God the Son, and God the Holy Spirit that we will reap the harvest of eternal life.

This should be the desire for all of God's created beings, but un-fortunately many drop by the wayside and never get to enjoy the peace and comfort that comes with obedience to the calling of God, for all are called, but only a few respond to that calling, are you one of the respondents or are you opening yourself to the condemnation of God?

I BELIEVE

I believe in Jesus Christ, I believe that Jesus is the Son of God, I believe in a Triune God; God the Father, God the Son, and God the Holy Spirit.

I believe that God through Jesus Christ created all that there is, from the smallest particle to the great mountains and the vastness of the seas was created to benefit you and me.

I believe that God sent His only Son, Jesus Christ, to earth to save sinners such as you and me from the fires of hell.

I believe that all who give their lives over to Jesus Christ and accept Him as their Lord and Savior will spend eternity with him when this world they leave.

I am not worthy to be called a child of God, I pray that He will accept me just as I am, my best is as filthy rags in His sight and yet He loves me and wants me to spend eternity with Him.

As much as I strive to fulfill His will in my life I fall short in many ways, I can only see today, Jesus sees beyond today and knows all from our beginning to our end and wants to share His eternal love with the likes of you and me.

Jesus Christ is my redeemer, He gave his all on the cross at Calvary so that all who come to believe in Him will be washed clean in His shed blood, our sins He will remember no more if we will but put our trust in Him.

I seek His guidance and pray that Jesus will soon return to earth and put an end to all the suffering and pain, that He will establish His kingdom here on earth and bring peace between all nations, great and small.

Jesus' "Light" shines on the path that He wants us to follow, all other paths lead to the pits of hell, only through following Jesus' ways can we become fit to spend eternity in His presence, He encourages one and all to come to Him.

When the dark clouds of temptations tempt you to stray turn your thoughts towards Jesus and He will give you the strength to resist those temptations, thus avoiding the consequences of falling prey to the temptations of the evil one.

I believe that even Satan is subservient to Jesus Christ and can only tempt us to stray, it is you and me who accepts the temptations of Satan and fall short of what God has in store for those who put Jesus first in their lives.

Believe in our Triune God and live, follow Satan and die.

I WANT TO GO HOME

I want to go home Mamma; I want to see Grandma and Grandpa,
I hear them calling my name Mamma.

I want to see Uncle Bob and Aunt May Mamma; I want to go home,
I dreamed of them last night Mamma and they called my name.

Is it time Mamma, is it time for me to go home Mamma, my bags are
all packed Mamma, is it time to go Mamma?

Wait a while son, don't leave me just yet, I'm not ready to let you go
son, let us reckon on this awhile.

But Mamma, I hear the Lord calling my name Mamma, what am I to
tell him Mamma?

Tell him son that Uncle Phil needs you to help on the farm or that
Aunt Flo is sick and needs you son, I'm not ready to
let you go.

Please Mamma, let me go, the pain is so bad Mamma, I needs to go
Mamma, tell Papa goodbye for me Mamma.

I will miss you son, tell them all that your Mamma understands, go
my son, tell the Lord that Mamma said to take good care
of you, you hear?

Goodbye Mamma, I'll tell them all what you said Mamma. With that
little Johnny died in his Mamma's arms.

There was a note that little Johnny had left and it read, "It's time
Mamma, it's time for me to go home, I heard the Lord calling my
name Mamma. I'm not afraid Mamma and don't be you."
signed, Johnny.

IN THE FULLNESS OF TIME

God is preparing his followers to occupy the new kingdom to come. When the time is right, (then and only then) will He allow Jesus to return to this earth and gather His Church unto Himself.

We all have the opportunity of becoming one of those who will become a member of his Church; there will be only a few who choose to do so. Far too many choose to cling to materialism and enjoy the things of the flesh, even more prefer to stay in sin and refuse to work towards such a goal. They want their pleasures here and now, rather than laying up treasures in heaven, where they will get to enjoy those treasures once they pass from this life to eternal life. This life being like a wisp of smoke that disappears from view when the winds blow, eternal life is forever, throughout all of eternity, of which there is no end.

For one to become a member of God's Church they must submit completely to the will of God, even to the point of going through many and varied hardships. To the giving up of family if, that is what God decreases. One cannot give up or change only that which he wants; they must follow the dictates of God completely. It takes a lot of trust and faith to follow God, but one must have such trust and faith in God if they ever hope to be with God for eternity.

One cannot keep one foot in materialism and one foot in spiritualism, for doing so one will fail to meet the qualifications of becoming a resident in God's kingdom.

God will never ask someone to do something that they are not capable of doing; He will also provide the means for one to carry out His will. Trials are meant to bring one closer to God and in doing so, ones faith and trust in God grows. At the time, some of these trials may seem impossible to endure, but through faith and prayer, one can and will endure. Turning to God can make all the difference in the world.

The rewards for following God and doing His will will be far beyond ones expectations. There are only two places where one will go after leaving this life, one is to become a member of God's Church in heaven and the other is to spend eternity in the lake of fire that burns with brimstone, separated from God for eternity. Man is not the one who makes the final decision as to where he will spend eternity; God Himself has given Jesus Christ that position. Jesus will give everyone the opportunity to follow Him, but in no way will He force anyone to do so. It is man's free choice as to where he will spend eternity.

God does not want to lose any of His children and He will be saddened every time one of them is lost. There will be much rejoicing in heaven when one of God's children makes the decision to follow His ways. Regardless of where one lives or their financial or social standing might be, God loves them and will only turn His head from them when they choose to follow Satan and live in sin.

There is much in this life to enjoy without losing the love of God. This world that God created for man is wonderfully made and full of priceless treasures. One of the greatest treasures that God created is the family. Materialism will never take the place of the family, even though it helps to support the family. All of God's creation was created for the benefit of man. Man was and is meant to control and care for God's creation. When man allows materialism to control him, then he is in danger of the judgment of God.

There will be many who apply to be members of God's Church, but there will be only a few who will be accepted. Slowly but surely the Church of God will be filled, all will be faithful and righteous and fulfill all of the requirements of membership. One day Jesus Christ will return to be the head of God's Church, the timing of this event is known to God and God alone. Many have tried to predict this event and have fallen short every time. In God's time Jesus Christ will fulfill God's will and return to Earth and become the head of God's Church. Be ye therefore prepared, be not like the virgins who had no oil for their lamps and missed the opportunity of becoming a member of God's Church.

IN THE SHADOW
OF THE CROSS

Because I live in the shadow of the cross I have a tomorrow.

Yesterday is gone, tomorrow is my future and I will live it for the one who died in my place on the cross at Calvary.

Therein lays my gratitude, for Jesus nullified my sins as he gave His life for you and me.

O how fortunate we are to have someone love us so much that He gave His life so that we may have a new tomorrow.

Only the Son of God could show that much love, my soul rejoices every time I pause and bring His name to mind.

Tomorrow, yes there will be a tomorrow for all who turn from their sinful ways and kneel before the cross and turn their life over to Jesus.

Jesus' sacrifice on the cross has covered our sins of yesterday, today and tomorrow and He gives us to a new tomorrow, every day.

I can now see beyond today and will rejoice in a sin free tomorrow, one made possible by the one who gave His life so that you and I might live with Him forever on the other side of death's door.

His name is Jesus Christ, the Son of God, the Savior of the world, the Messiah, the Lord of lords and King of kings.

In him and through Him we shall live to see a new tomorrow, free from the sins that bind us if only we will come to Him and live in the shadow of the cross.

INDIVIDUALISM

The soul is independent from the flesh and in no way can the flesh or fleshly things of this world enter into the kingdom of God. Those who enter into the kingdom of God do so in the spirit and as individuals, not as a brother, sister or even a twin, for no two people are the same. Neither do we enter as a mother nor a father, for being a mother or a father is the means by which we can bring individuals into this fleshly world. We are all born into this world through earthly patents. We enter into the kingdom of God as spirits, devoid of all earthly ties.

Science is trying to clone people and have them alike in every respect. This theory is flawed because no matter how hard man tries to clone perfection he cannot do so. God created us as individuals with differing characteristics and in no way can man improve on what God has created. One excuse for cloning is that they hope to harvest different parts of the clone for transplantation purposes. Thus prolonging the lives of those who can afford such procedures, with disregard for the life of the clone.

We often say that we are brought up in the shadow of this person or that person, therefore implying that we are almost as good as that person, but perhaps lack their intelligence, therefore we are not quite as good as they are. God created us all equal, but not the same, everybody is different one from the other, and no two people are alike. We are judged on our own merits and stand accountable for our own actions, not someone who may look like us.

We are individuals regardless of our relationship one to the other, we think differently and act differently as individuals, and this carries through in every respect of our lives. When one tries to impose their ways upon another, this cause conflict and if not resolved, it can lead to greater conflict until it flames into war between nations and or ethnic groups. Is not this, which is going on today?

There is however a solution to all of man's differences and can change all into loving and caring people, willing to step forward and help their neighbor without expecting anything in return or raising arms against them. Turn to God and apply His laws to all situations and those differences will be overcome without conflict and all parties will live with one another in harmony and peace. God has the answer to all of man's problems if only man will give up pride and conduct himself as a one who has truly repented and seeks only to do God's will.

To those who refuse to change and hold to their old ways of life by putting earthly treasures before their love for God will die in their own sins and wonder why they have to suffer the fires of hell when they die. When death occurs it is too late make any changes in one's life, the die has been cast. God judges what is in one's heart, not how much wealth or how much power or prestige one might have. Nothing can be hidden from God, nor can God be manipulated. He knows all things every person on the face of the earth does and how they believe in regards as to

His Son, Jesus Christ. God judges on what is in one's heart, not their pocketbook. His judgments are just and His decisions are irreversible. Stand vigilant as to how you live and whom you worship. Harbor not hostilities and speak sweet words out of the mouth. They are a dead giveaway as to how one thinks and how they live. God knows all and will judge accordingly.

We can neither add nor take away from that which God has set before us. We can cover it with muck and mire, but when the showers from heaven come, it is as pure gold, un-scathed by the will of man. God respects no man, nor will He tolerate the breaking of his laws without punishment. It is not what you have or who you are that determines your future it is what is in your heart that God looks at. One can overcome sin through genuine repentance and thus be acceptable in His sight. Stand guard over your thoughts and deeds. Avoid evil, live in peace with your neighbor, and reap the rewards of heaven, rather than those of hell.

IS IT WELL WITH THY SOUL

Is it well with thy soul, have you taken the Holy Scriptures to heart and made them a part of your daily living?

Do you practice what you believe; have you changed your lifestyle to conform to the teachings of Jesus Christ?

When was the last time you bowed your knees before the throne of God and asked forgiveness of your sins and then turned your life over to Him or have you just gone about your life as usual?

Jesus Christ is knocking at your door, open it and receive the greatest gift that you will ever receive an invitation to spend eternity in the presence of the one who created you, Jesus Christ.

Everybody has either received or will receive an invitation to the wedding feast of the Lord, your invitation can be found in the pages of Scripture, all are invited but only a few will accept that invitation, for on the most part man does not want to give up the luxuries of life in favor of the possibility of being persecuted for ones faith.

They lack the moral courage to be different than what the world offers, they fear being ridiculed and set apart and in some cases put to death for their belief.

How strange for whether one acknowledges Jesus Christ as Lord and Savior or not they will one day die anyway, why not die knowing that you will spend eternity with Jesus Christ and avoid the possibility of being condemned to spend eternity in hell.

Jesus Christ is a loving God and will without question take all unto Himself who come to Him and accept Him as their God and Lord of all.

Jesus is waiting, now is the time and place to put aside earthly desires and turn from our wicked ways and seek the mercy of God and his offer of salvation, His offer will always be there, it is you and me who has to change, not God.

If man stubbornly stands in his pagan ways and turns his back on God, Jesus Christ and the Holy Spirit he will live to regret such a decision, for the day is fast approaching when Jesus Christ will return to earth and establish His kingdom here on earth and at that time all knees will bow before His throne and declare that He is Lord of all, then those who reject Jesus as their sovereign God will be cast into the fires of hell, there suffer the consequences of their decision.

Is it well with thee or are you one of those who thinks that God will not condemn anyone to hell, well, you would be right to think so, you see, it is not God who condemns man to hell, it is man who condemns himself to hell by rejecting the loving overtures of God and His offer of salvation, He is just carrying out our wishes, in other words we condemn ourselves to hell, not God.

Turn your life over to God while it is still day, for the night approaches when no one will be able to change their heart and ways of thinking, God is the judge of whether we have changed or not, for He knows and sees what is in the heart of man and He will judge man accordingly, like the hymn asks, "Is it well with thy soul?"

IT'S TIME

I pray for the day almighty God that Your Son, Jesus Christ will grace our sky, that He will scatter the seeds of love and that to fertile ground they will fly.

Let it be so Lord that His footprints lead His followers to new heights where their souls can flourish and never die.

From early sun, until darkness fills the sky may He walk among His sheep and guard them from the evil eye.

Hold us Lord close to Your side, shelter us so there we may feed on nectar from on high, that we may grow in Thy word and be a friend to those with whom we abide.

Lord, grant that this day will soon arrive and bring peace to the troubled souls that now wrestle with the temptations of life here on earth.

Fill their hearts with love and let them see beyond tomorrow to a new day, a new life, a new mission to fulfill their lives.

When this earth quakes and the fires burn our earthly homes lift us above the turmoil and strife, that we may rest in Your arms until Your will is complete.

Then release us that we may replenish Your new world with those who will bend their knee before Your throne and forever be free to worship Thee.

We await O Lord for what is yet to come, a day You promised eons ago, in Your time may it be fulfilled and bring peace to those who seek to do Thy will.

As my forefathers before me, I bow before Thy throne and commit my life to fulfilling what You would have me to do.

Most of all Lord I pray that the time is near when the clouds of the sky gather and we hear the sound of the trumpets announce the coming of Your Son, our Lord and Savior to vanquish sin from our lives.

Thank You Lord for listening to my prayer, may it come to be that you will grant Your children a place in Your new world to come. Come Lord Jesus, Come.

JESUS CHRIST IS LORD AND SAVIOR

J— Jesus Christ is Lord and creator of all.

E— Eternity with God is available to all. Where will you spend eternity?

S— Some will spend eternity in the presence of God; others will spend eternity in hell.

U— Until you turn to Jesus for forgiveness you will remain trapped in sin.

S— Saying you are a Christian without living as one is hypocrisy.

C— Come before the throne of God and commit your life to His service.

H— How is your relationship with God, is it as the Bible requires?

R— Real commitment to God requires us to put Him first in our lives.

I— In time all will bow before the throne of God and declare Him Lord of all.

S— Some think they can live as they please and still spend eternity with God.

T— Time is running out, now is the time to turn one's life over to God, not tomorrow.

I— In time all will come to know Jesus Christ as Lord and Savior.

S— Sin is a stumbling block and can only be overcome through Jesus Christ.

L— Loving your neighbor as yourself is the key to forgiveness.

O—Only by accepting Jesus Christ as our Lord and Savior can we be saved.

R— Ready or not one day all will stand before God and make an account for how they lived their lives here on earth.

D—Death is inevitable, are you ready?

A— Always be ready to give your personal testimony as to how Jesus has changed your life.

N— Nearer and nearer we come to Jesus Christ as we study the Bible and apply it to our lives.

D—Do you want to change and find it hard, keep praying and hold fast to that which is good as found in the Bible.

S— Save time every day to study the Bible and pray for those in need.

A— Angles are messengers from God and will bring comfort with their presence.

V— Victory over death comes to those who turn to God and allow Him to guide then on their path of life.

I— Instead of trying to justify your way of life submit to God and see the difference it will make in your life.

O—Only those who accept Jesus Christ as their Lord and Savior shall look upon the face of God.

R— Right now is the time to turn one's life over to Jesus Christ, tomorrow may be too late.

JESUS IS CALLING

Make room for Jesus in your heart, make Him the cornerstone of your foundation of life, turn to Him when in need, and praise Him as you travel your road of life.

Jesus came so that we may have life and have it more abundantly, Jesus is life itself and all that goes with it.

Jesus Christ, the Son of God as revealed by the Holy Scriptures created all things, even life itself.

When the dark clouds of sin roll in Jesus' "Light" will shines through and reveal the path that leads to freedom from sin.

Yes, it is Jesus whom we should follow, declare that His way is for you and fear not what Satan can do.

Satan offers temporary gratification, Jesus offers eternal peace and righteousness and withholds not from those who follow Him.

Now is the time to change ones course in life, Jesus is calling, listen and one can hear Him calling from the cross of Calvary.

While on the cross Jesus opened the door to eternal life, and will shut it not, those who hear will come and commit their lives to His service, all others are condemned already.

Join hands at the foot of the cross, answer with one voice, "We accept thy offer of eternal life O Lord. Lead us on to victory."

"Surly goodness and mercy shall follow us the rest of the days of our lives and we will dwell with Thee throughout eternity."

Jesus is in control of all things, never will He leave us alone, Jesus offers comfort to all who turn to Him, never will Satan be able to break the bond between Jesus and those who accept Him as the cornerstone of their life.

Jesus is calling, calling to those who will listen and obey, "Come unto me and I will give thee rest and make you one of mine. Follow Me and I will give you the final victory."

JESUS IS KNOCKING ON YOUR DOOR

We are sojourners here on earth with but one place to go, towards the door of death, one-day at a time.

As we approach our hour of death we become acutely aware that we have a choice to make, either to say, "Lord, I am ready to face eternity with you", or plead for more time because you have been too busy fulfilling your earthly desires.

Ready or not death will come and after passing through the door of death, the path splits and goes in two different directions. One has a sign over it that says, "All who have accepted my Son, Jesus Christ as their Lord and Savior follow this path." Over the other path is a sign that reads, "All others go this way." Those who hear the voice of the Great Shepherd follow the path to eternal life. Those who have followed the voice of Satan follow the path to eternal damnation.

It is before we pass through the door of death that we have the opportunity to prepare for eternal life by self-sacrifice and spending our time learning about and applying the truths of God to our lives as found in the Holy Scriptures.

Those who spend their time seeking the pleasures of the flesh with disregard for where they will spend eternity are those who have no choice but to follow the sign that reads, "All others go this way." We seek that which we want for ourselves, often times not realizing that our future abode will be determined by how we conduct ourselves throughout our lives.

Death of the flesh cannot be avoided, but eternal damnation can be avoided by turning to Jesus Christ now and asking Him to come into our life and submitting to His will rather than our own will. No matter what the sin may be, Jesus will forgive it if we confess it and seek His forgiveness.

Jesus knocks on your door of life, open it and embrace Him as you walk ever closer to the door of death, for once death occurs it is too late to change your mind. Know before you die where you will spend eternity, it is all laid out in the Holy Scriptures. Once death occurs, it is too late to change.

Now, today, this very hour is the time to accept Jesus Christ as your Lord and Redeemer. Let go of earthly pleasures, for they have only one end, eternal damnation. Seek the Lord while it is still day, for the night fast approaches when no man can see where he is going. Death draws nigh.

JESUS OUR SAVIOR

Just as Jesus was sent from God, so do we come from God. The difference being that Jesus is the Son of God and we are but a reflection of Jesus. When Jesus was born of woman, He was incorruptible and remained incorruptible through out His earthly journey. When we were born, we were corruptible, for we were born in sin and Jesus knew no sin. The sin of man came about when Eve fell to the temptation of Satan in the Garden of Eden.

Jesus was sent into this world by God to be a sacrifice for the sins of the whole world and through Him; all may come to repentance and be saved. Jesus suffered all things for us, even the brutality of the cross, where He suffered the penalty for your sins and mine. Jesus knew that His mission in this world was to do His Father's will and in so doing He opened the door to eternal life for all who come to believe. Jesus offers salvation as a free gift to all who accept Him as who He claims to be, the Son of God.

Most walk blindly through this life never caring that much about God or their future beyond the grave. We become so entangled in achieving earthly things that we cannot see beyond our own wants and fall deeper and deeper into sin and the materialistic things of this life, oh what fools we become. Material things cannot take the place of Spiritual things if one ever expects to have a good spiritual life. We came into this life with nothing and we will leave this life with nothing, but oh, how we try to fulfill our every desire for materialism.

There are no more joyous words to utter than, "Once I was blind, but now I see." This can come about through the study of God's word and applying then to our lives, leaving earthly things behind and looking towards the goal of becoming an active child of God, working for the advancement of His kingdom here on earth. We will never become perfect, but we can work towards that end by committing ourselves to his service. Jesus admonishes us to put off the old man and put on the new man and to take up our cross, follow Him, and become as little children for such is the kingdom of God.

When age overtakes you, remember how you believed everything your parents told you just because they were your mother and father. Therefore, must we in older age revert to our childhood faith and believe every word that proceeds from the mouth of God. God is our true Father and as a loving, Father He will walk with us as we make our way through this life and be as a "Light" unto our path. Those who have had a personal encounter with Jesus Christ find it easier to believe in and trust in Jesus Christ than those who have never had such an experience. As the Bible declares, great is the faith of those who have seen, but greater yet is the faith of those who have not seen and yet believe.

Remember it is Satan who tempts us to stray as we walk our road of life, not God. Through Jesus Christ, we can learn how to resist these temptations by putting on the full armor of God and standing fast in His Son, Jesus Christ. Jesus gave us permission to use His name against Satan in our struggle against evil and that by doing so we can overcome evil with good. The temptations of Satan only have the power over us as we allow them to have. God told Satan, "Thus far and no further." In other words, Satan only has the power of temptation, not the power of death and destruction as many think. We ourselves give Satan power over us to cause us to destroy ourselves. Read the book of Job.

Throw off the old man, put on the new, and become as little children trusting in Jesus Christ the one who can save us from ourselves and the temptations of this materialistic world. Stand in His "Light" and rejoice in it, praising God from whom all blessings flow. In Him is no darkness at all and again rejoice.

JESUS SET ME FREE

As I walked by Calvary that faithful day, I had the
urge to lay my labors aside.

Up the hill I climbed and found Jesus nailed to a
Roman cross, my soul was heavy with the
sin I carried inside.

In prayer I kneeled before Him and asked God to
forgive a sinner such as me and to release
Jesus from that cross.

To which He replied, "My Son is paying the price
for your sins this day. Go, you are free from
the bondage of your sinful ways."

As the blood of Jesus struck the ground I felt a
great weight being lifted from my shoulders.

Tears began to flow as I kneeled there before my
dying Savior, it was I who belonged on
that cross, not He.

With a prayer of thanks I rose from the ground and
joined hands with the others who witnessed
the death of Jesus that day.

With His last breath, Jesus declared, "It is finished."
then He bowed His head and died.

With tears on my cheeks I said my goodbyes and turned towards home.

Yes, Jesus set me free the day I turned aside and climbed the hill at Calvary.

JESUS' GUIDING "LIGHT"

Jesus is a "Light" unto our path. His "Light" can guide us through the shallow waters of life where our ship of life can flounder on the rocks of sin and be lost. His "Light" is as a beacon and will never be extinguished. It may not always be visible to us, but it is still there and will guide all who seek Him. As we wander through the shallow waters of life without a beacon to guide us, we can be caught up in the currents of sin that leads to destruction.

If we close our eyes and wander around in the darkness, we stumble and fall, so will a ship that has no rudder wallow in the seas, and sink because of its inability to face the storms head on. So it is with us if we do not have any sense of direction, we will be swamped by the trials of life and not survive. It takes a strong hand on the tiller and a weathered eye on the distant beacon of "light" (Jesus Christ) in order to guide our ship of life through the storms of life. Hesitate not to ask Jesus for directions when your eyes become blurred from the strain of trying to do your thing without the support of that guiding "Light". We, like the ship will soon sink without a proper guidance system. A guidance system that only Jesus Christ can provide, it is there for all to seek.

The "Light" of Jesus Christ transcends time and space and can never be extinguished, no matter who or what tries to dull its guiding "Light". This "Light" shines in the darkest of places and nullifies the efforts of our adversary, Satan, in his efforts to distract us from our pilgrimage to the throne of God.

Like a ship on a storm tossed sea without a rudder to guide it we will soon become lost and succumb to the fury of the storm, so will we become lost in the darkness of the abyss of sin without the "Light" of Jesus Christ to guide us. Jesus' "Light" is capable of shinning in the darkness of sin and leading the lost back to the peace and quiet of homeport, in the presence of God.

Seek the guiding "Light" of Jesus Christ and fear not for your safety, for as long as you seek the "Light" of Jesus Christ He will be as a rudder to your ship of life and guide you to safe harbors. Like the Good Shepherd, that Jesus is He will be as a guiding "Light" to all who seek shelter from the temptations of Satan. Our fight is with the forces of darkness (Satan and his fallen angels), they would have us turn from the "Light" and fall into the abyss of sin, for Satan's objective is to lead all of God's children astray that he can. Open your heart and allow the "Light" of Jesus Christ to shine therein and lead you to the protective harbor of God's love.

The day fast approaches when the "Light" of life, Jesus Christ, will overcome all sin, and sin will never again be a stumbling block to all who believe. Satan and all who proclaim his way of life will be cast into the lake of fire from which there is no return. Satan is well aware of where he will be spending eternity and in his rage, he is trying to take as many of God's people with him as he possibly can through deception. Stand fast in God's word and avoid becoming one of Satan's victims.

Whether we be like the ship on the storm tossed sea without a rudder or like the lost soul in the desert of sin we all need the "Light" of Jesus Christ to comfort us and take away all of our fears and guide us on our road of life. By standing fast in the "Light" of Jesus Christ, we will be equipped to withstand the temptations of Satan that can lead to spending eternity in the lake of fire. The "Light" of life frees us from all sin, open the door when you hear Jesus knocking on your door and invite Him to be your Lord and Savior. Jesus is the lamp that will never go out, nor will His "Light" ever dim. It will shine from everlasting to everlasting and forever be as a guiding "Light" to all who proclaim Him as King of kings and Lord of lords.

JESUS' LOVE FOR YOU AND ME

To Him go when your day goes astray and He will reply, "Hold fast, tell me your problems and I will help you overcome."

This proved His love for you and me, now we know for sure that we can go to Him when in need.

He is gentle, His eyes are soft, His voice is comforting and He consoles us every day.

He holds our hand and helps us walk the path of righteousness so that we will not succumb to the temptations that besiege us.

He loves us whether our days are of sunshine or rain, we bend our knees before him when it is time to pray.

We love to watch Him when He heals the infirmities of those who seek His ways.

He may scold us, but he will never say, "Go away, do not bother me today."

Instead, to our delight He will heal us when a fevered brow we have.

When times are hard and food is scarce, He will open His warehouse and shower us with all of our needs.

The day is coming when the heavens will open and we will see Jesus as He sits upon His throne, smiling and welcoming those who have accepted Him as King of kings and Lord of lords.

In Him, we can find comfort when things go astray, through this He shows his love for you and me.

Jesus freed us from the bondage of sin when upon the cross of Calvary He hung, He died so that you and I could have eternal life.

His "Light" shines upon all, it reminds us to keep our eyes on Him and keep walking in his ways.

Turn to Jesus in prayer and thank Him for all that He has done for sinners such as you and me.

JESUS, THE DOOR TO ETERNAL LIFE

In chapter three in the book of John Jesus answered Nicodemus' question of how one can be born again when he is old by saying in verse five; Jesus answered, Verily, verily, I say unto thee, Except a man be born of water and of the Spirit, he cannot enter into the kingdom of God. Also in the book of John, chapter fourteen verses five and six we read; Thomas saith unto Him, Lord, we know not whither thou goest; and how can we know the way? Jesus saith unto him, I am the way, the truth, and the life: no man cometh unto the Father, but by me. In chapter, fourteen in the book of John we read in verse one; Let not your heart be troubled: ye believe in God, believe also in me. (KJV) In essence, Jesus was saying that He (Jesus) is the door to eternal life and that no one can enter into the kingdom of God except through Him.

Through these verses, Jesus establishes His authority as the Son of God and that He is the door to eternal life and that all other doors lead to separation from God for eternity.

There are those who believe whole heartily in God and yet reject Jesus Christ as being the one and only Son of God. They have established their own set of rules as to who can and cannot enter into the presence of God and all others are as dogs needing to be killed because they do not believe as they do.

Then there are those who believe that if they do enough good deeds that a loving God will not reject them when they die, but rather welcome them into His presence for all time. In the meantime, they live life their way with little or no thought that they should apply all of the scriptures to their own lives, rather than those they choose to follow.

Others interpret and change the meaning of the scriptures to say that they are the only ones who will enter into the kingdom of God and all others will perish in the fires of hell. They too interpret the Holy Scriptures to suit themselves and often establish that their leader is in fact the chosen one of God and therefore he cannot be wrong.

Many are following false gods and trying to impose their ways and thoughts on the rest of the world. Teaching that their way is the only way to achieve eternal life. When in fact the Holy Scriptures from Genesis to Revelation clearly establishes that Jesus Christ in fact is the one and only Son of God and that He and He alone has the authority to say who can and cannot enter into the kingdom of God.

It is also clear through the Scriptures that God has given man the choice as to how he wants to live, whom he wants to worship, and how he wants to believe, and that he God may not agree with that choice but will respect that choice. Thus as individuals we have the right to think, believe, and live the way that pleases us without regard for what the Holy Scriptures have to say. Though God allows man that privilege, He (God) has set the parameters in the Holy Scriptures by which man has to live if he decides that he wants to spend eternity in the presence of God and from that, there is no deviation.

Jesus spoke about dying, heaven and hell more than He did about any other subject. Jesus came and lived among His creation to bring the good news of salvation and that through Him we can enter into the kingdom of God when we leave this world behind. Again, Jesus has left that decision up to each individual.

If one accepts one verse or even one word in the Holy Scriptures as being true then they must accept all of the Holy Scriptures as being true. On the other hand, if they reject one word of the Holy Scriptures as being false then they are calling God a liar and declaring that God has no authority to set the standards of who can or cannot enter into His kingdom. They are also declaring that they know more than God knows and will live life any way they choose without consequences. When in fact there are consequences for our actions whether they are for the good or the bad. These consequences will be metered out when one by one we stand before the judgment seat of God.

I leave you with this. What if you are wrong to assume that the Holy Scriptures are wrong or a false theology? Would it not be prudent to err on the side that all of the Holy Scriptures are true rather than just a few chosen books or verses? What do you say?

Are you willing to risk where you will spend eternity if you are wrong?

John five, verse twenty four reads; Verily, verily, I say unto you, He that heareth my word and believeth on him that sent me, hath everlasting life, and shall not come into condemnation; but is passed from death unto life. (KJV)

JUST A REFLECTION

O Lord I have no power, knowledge, nor life, only that which
You give unto me.

I can do nothing of myself, for I am weak and helpless, lost
in this materialistic world.

I depend upon you Lord Jesus for the very breath that
nourishes my body. My mind cannot function
without the love that flows from you.

I am incapable of controlling my own life without Your
guiding hand, a hand that will never be withdrawn
as long as I live according to You.

Thou have supplied me with all of my needs, my store-
house overflows with your abundance.

Even the sun cannot shine upon this world (Your creation)
without Your consent.

The moon and stars shine at night to remind us of Your
great power, power to create any and all things
that You have made.

Given without strings attached, nor have you restricted
us in our use of Your gifts, for nothing was made
that You did not make.

Many of us wander through this life not knowing where
we came from or where we are going.

Lost in a sea of strangers, never acknowledging Thee and
yet You still love us and care for us as though
we had never strayed from Thee.

We do not deserve to be one of Your children and yet You are
not willing that even one of us should be lost. How
much greater love can we have than that.

Thy words, works and deeds have been written in a great book
that we call the "Holly Bible" and as great a book that
it is, it just covers a portion of Your love
for mankind.

There is so much more for us to know about Thee O Lord, that
a lifetime is not long enough to learn it all.

We have but scratched the surface of Your love for us, but even
this limited knowledge is sufficient to sustain us
until we join Thee in the afterlife.

We are but a reflection of what we will become when we leave
this life and are transformed into a likeness of Thee.

JUST FOR YOU AND ME

Jesus took our place on the cross at Calvary, to Him we owe.

With love in His heart for sinners like you and me He set us free.

Without hesitation Jesus stepped forward and took our sins upon Himself and bore our penalty.

We owe Jesus a debt of gratitude, one that we can never pay without going to Him and offering ourselves in service to Him.

This is our calling, to let go of our earthly ties and serve Him wherever He directs us to go.

It is for us to take up our cross and follow Jesus and let the rest of the world know that He is our Lord and Savior.

To die to self and serve Jesus is what we are called to do; our lives belong to Him and Him we ought to obey.

Tomorrow may be too late to surrender to Jesus. He calls us to surrender today while we still have the light of day.

Jesus took our place on the cross of Calvary, to Him we owe.

We will sing praises unto Jesus as we turn from our wicked ways and start our lives anew.

Our names are now written in the Lamb's book of Life, this we know because Jesus promised that all who believe in Him shall inherit eternal life.

JUST SOME THOUGHTS

Though the earth's surface is covered mostly with water, God's love covers the whole world and is directed towards all people, not just a select few.

*   *   *

God holds His entire creation in the palm of His hand; at his whim He can do with it as pleases Him.

*   *   *

Forgiveness frees the soul to praise God, unforgiveness binds the soul and it decays and dies.

*   *   *

Revenge is as a noose around ones throat; it suffocates forgiveness and hardens ones soul.

*   *   *

Sowing love takes the burden from ones shoulders and reaches out with compassion towards those who offend you.

*   *   *

It is God within us that gives us the desire to forgive, not we ourselves.

* * *

We are the temple of God, we are also the temple's keeper, we either reflect God's "Light" and His love or we extinguish His "Light" and withhold His love.

* * *

We reflect our inner feelings and thoughts by the way we treat our fellowman, we either reflect God or we reflect Satan.

* * *

Today is the day to forgive, tomorrow may be too late, for once death comes all is sealed and cannot be changed.

* * *

Would you rather be counted among the wheat or the tares, the wheat shall bring forth much fruit, the tares shall be cast into the ever consuming fires of hell.

* * *

It is better to die a pauper and submit to the will of God than it is to have all the wealth in the world and have it as a millstone around ones neck.

*   *   *

It is not our place to run the world, it is our place to submit to the will of God and let Him run the world through us.

LAST CHANCE

Through the power of temptation Satan entices many to go astray with the promise of wealth, social standing, personal gratification, positions of power, and many other enticing acts that when acted upon puts the recipient under the control of Satan. Whether they realize it or not they are blind to the truth as taught in the Holy Scriptures, they see only what pleases them and fulfills their earthly desires. To be under the control of Satan is to become spiritually dead and the forfeiting of eternal life, thus being under the condemnation of spending eternity in hell. Satan and his fallen angels are a powerful force in the materialistic world and yet he himself along with his fallen angels are already condemned to spend eternity in the lake of fire where the worm never dies. Jesus Christ defeated Satan when He stated, "It is finished." while upon the cross of Calvary. This was Satan's death-knell and sentence will be executed after the second coming of Jesus Christ.

All have sinned and fallen short of the glory of God. As humans, we are weak and susceptible to the temptations of Satan. Even though one may have fallen prey to the temptations of Satan and are under his control does not mean that they have to remain under his control and be condemned to hell. Turning from sin and seeking the forgiveness of sin comes when one realizes that sin does not fulfill the desires of their heart and is a dead-end road. Sin leaves one empty inside without hope for a better future. It can be a struggle to make the necessary changes, but through fervent prayer and supplication change for the better will come to all who come before the throne of Jesus Christ seeking His forgiveness. Jesus offers redemption to all who come before Him, seek forgiveness of their sins, and through His forgiveness, restored to their rightful place in His redeemed flock.

God has prepared two places for us to spend eternity. The first is a new heaven and a new earth, only those whose names are written in the Book of Life shall enter therein. This includes those who have accepted Jesus Christ as the Son of God and their Lord and Savior and have made Jesus head of their household. There is much rejoicing in heaven every time someone turns their life over to Jesus and accepts Him as their Lord and Savior.

The second is the Lake of Fire; this is reserved for all who reject Jesus Christ and live life their way. We condemn ourselves to eternal damnation when we disregard our spiritual life in favor of the material things of life. Many fool themselves by declaring that there is no life after death and live life accordingly. Their vision is fine and yet they are blind to the spiritual aspect of life and the consequences of living an agnostic life. God so loves us that He will honor whichever way of life we choose to live, but this does not negate the consequences of living a life of agnosticism. This situation can be reversed by turning to Jesus Christ and asking Him to come into one's live and allowing Jesus to become the center of their lives.

The biggest obstacle keeping the unbeliever from becoming a child of God is self and not wanting to give up control over their lives to a deity that they can neither see nor touch. They put materialism and what it can do for them above the spiritual side of life and live life to satisfy themselves rather than live life by a set of laws that restricts them from seeking the pleasures that are contrary to a Christ-like life. Broad is the way and wide is the gate that leads to self-destruction and eternal damnation. Narrow is the way and narrow is the gate that leads to eternal life. No one is perfect nor will anyone ever be perfect, all have fallen short of the glory of God. It is only through Jesus Christ and His sacrificial act of paying the price of your sins and mine on the cross of Calvary that any of us can be saved, fit to enter the kingdom of God.

The future of those who have come to believe in Jesus Christ and live life accordingly is as bright as the morning star; all others will be condemned to hell. It is in here in this life that each of us determines where we will spend eternity. Change can come about right up to the time we take our last breath, but after that moment, it is too late to change. Many a deathbed conversion has been witnessed; an expression of thankfulness and love was on the face of the dying. This life is the last chance one will ever have to come before the throne of God and turn their life over to Him, acknowledging His Son, Jesus Christ as their Lord and Savior, thus assuring themselves eternal life.

LET IT BE SAID

I would like it be said of me that God saved him from spending eternity in hell when he turned from his disobedience ways and sought the solace of God, that he was an obedient child of God and that he allowed God to guide him on his road of life.

That he took up his cross and followed Jesus Christ, that he sought the comfort of God as he went through his trials of life and resisted the temptations of Satan by holding fast to the word of God.

Let it be said that he sought the comfort that God offers as the fires of life burned away the dross that brought him closer to God instead of seeking revenge for the wrongs that were imposed upon him.

That he humbled himself before the throne of God and thought of himself more of a servant of God, rather than one seeking glory for himself, of how honored he felt when God told him to take pen in hand and write that which He wanted him to say.

Of how humbly he walked before God and gave God all of the credit for his literary accomplishments, for he himself was unschooled in that field and wrote only that which God lead him to put on paper.

That he lived a long and fulfilling life, that he reached out to others through his writings and encouraged them to seek the word of God and apply it to their lives, for in the end that is all that really matters in this life.

If you would like these things to be said about you when you are gone then turn to God now and turn your life over to Him and allow Him to guide you on your road of life. Let God lead you to what He wants you to do rather than what you want. Become a servant of God rather than a servant of self-desire.

It is a matter of what one thinks is more important in life, fulfilling selfish desires or preparing oneself for the life that comes after the death of the body. Let it said of you that you were a faithful servant of the most high God.

I humbly offer this as a testimony of what God can do in one's life if they are willing to forego some of the pleasures of life and be obedient to God's calling. We are all called but only a few will answer.

LET THEM COME
FORTH

There are those who mutilate the unborn child and dismember them limb for limb, then suction the last drop of life from the womb of the mother and claim that there is no life in the unborn child. They have no regard for God or the life that that unborn child could have had. Their own desire is to do the work of Satan. They worship they know not what. They claim to love God and accept Jesus Christ as their Lord and they continue to slaughter the unborn. They hear not the cries of those who they dismember and cast into the garbage like so much unwanted trash.

Those who oppose abortion are looked upon as being right-wingers and out of touch with reality. The abortionist has sight and yet they are blind to what they are doing and cannot see beyond the scalpel they hold in their hand. They have ears and yet they hear not the cries of pain as they dismember the unborn. They believe that it is better to kill than it is to raise the unwanted child. Their motto is, get rid of the unborn before you are burdened down with a child that you do not want, kill it before you give yourself a chance to become attached to it.

The abortionist believes only that which is relevant to their cause, they cannot see beyond their selfish ideals and ignore the agony they cause. In time, these cries will come to haunt them and they will find no peace or be able to justify what they have done. They do not think that abortion is murder and it is only when they suffer themselves that they come to the realization that they are wrong. By this time, it is too late to reverse what they have done and the rest of their lives they will have to live with the carnage that they have caused.

The abortionist is like a slick-Willie and has all kinds of arguments for their way of thinking and have utter disregard for human life. The ones having the abortion condone abortion as a way of getting rid of an unwanted pregnancy and refuse to take responsibility of motherhood. Even in the case of incest and rape, the unborn still represents a human life and is just as precious in the eyes of God as the rest of us are. All aborted fetuses are just as human as you and I are; as such, they have the same rights as any of us have.

Life is a gift from God and deserves be treated as such. No one can terminate the life of an unborn and expect mercy from God. The Bible teaches that God knew us before we were in our mother's womb. If one believes in God and that the Bible is His holy word, then how can anyone kill and maim the unborn? Such decision to kill the unborn is of Satan and carries with it the death sentence of the soul (separated from God for eternity). The burden of taking an unborn life will be burdensome to the soul.

The abortionist seems to have the attitude that these unwanted babies do not deserve to live, therefore it is better to kill them than it is to raise them and give them the same opportunities in life that they had. They believe that it is better to kill than it is to raise a child that has a handicap and is not able to live as a productive person. They stand as judge, jury and executioner, backed up by the laws of man. They set themselves up as a god and take life from those who they do not think deserves life.

All unborn life represents children of God and as such deserves to be treated with respect and dignity. It is Satan who spreads this idea that some of us do not deserve to live. It is he who wants us to think just because someone might have a handicap that they do not have the right to live. As Christians, we are called upon to love those who take human life through abortion and pray for them to see the damage they are inflicting upon society and encourage them give up such practices. Those who walk in darkness need all of the love and support that they can get and as Christians, we are called upon to supply that love and support. We will be blessed many times over for reaching out in love to those who have disregard for life.

Life begins at the moment of conception and all of the arguing in the world will not change that fact. To destroy a human life, born or unborn will serve to destroy oneself, for one cannot take a life without taking on the consequences of such actions. Destroying the unborn destroys our future; our future depends upon those being born now. God is supreme and will judge all who go against His will. His judgment will be just.

LIFE AND TIME

Here on earth we are limited as to how far we can travel and where we can go. We are also limited by time, we only have so many years in which to accomplish what we want to do with our lives and we are limited to doing one thing at a time. These are all limitations imposed upon our human existence. Without limitations, we would be able to travel to all parts of God's creation without impunity. Perhaps one day we will be able to travel to distant planets or galaxies but for now we are limited to just our immediate surroundings.

One of our greatest constraints is time. It seems as though we are no more born than it is time to leave this life behind and enter into eternity. Where time is a constraint here on earth there is no time in eternity, just the ever present now. Eternity had no beginning nor does it have any end. Certainly, God knew what He was doing when He created heaven, earth, and all things therein, including time. Time is our way of measuring the length of time that something exists. Take away time and everything is endless, no beginning, no end.

This is the way that it is with God; God has always been and will always be, no beginning and no end. God created man to live forever and he shall. He put man here on earth to forever live in His presence, but when sin entered the life of man God put a limit as to how many years man (you and I) will live.

We find in the Bible that God granted man to live three score and ten years, many die long before their seventy years and many live beyond seventy years. This is one of the mysteries of God. However, man's body will die in its allotted time, but his soul shall live forever, either in the presence of God or in hell.

Man (you and I) do not have control over how many years we might live here on earth but we do have control of where we will spend eternity. Through the love that God has for all people of this earth He sent His one and only Son, Jesus Christ into this world so that all who come to believe in Him shall inherit eternal life. While here on earth, Jesus Christ gave his life on the cross of Calvary as a sacrifice for the sins of the whole world and through this sacrifice opened the door to eternal life, both a gift from God, free to all who accept Jesus Christ as their Lord and Savior.

You and I have the choice of accepting Jesus' offer of eternal life or rejecting his offer. We are free to pursue Jesus' offer of eternal life by turning our lives over to Him and let Him guide us through this life or we have the choice of rejecting Him and pursuing the riches, power and self-centeredness that this earthly life has to offer. Whichever decision we make Jesus will honor that decision, He is the one who offers a better way of life, it is you and me who chooses what we think is best for ourselves. We have up to the moment just before death to answer that question, once death occurs it is too late to choose or change our mind. We are responsible for our own decisions and we will be judged by them on that great Day of Judgment.

Time is of the essence; the life span of man (you and I) is so short that we have no time to prolong the decision of what we want, eternal life or residency in hell. Our lives are as the early morning mist, when the sun rises the mist is vaporized and seen no more, the only thing remaining might be a few dewdrops of moisture on leaves or vegetation. Therefore, the only thing that we can leave is our legacy of how we lived our lives here on earth and how many other lives we touched. Be wise in the decisions that you make during your lifetime, your future residency depends upon it.

LIFE CHANGING
DECISIONS

I urge you my fellow travelers, read the Scriptures, search them and draw your own conclusion whether they are true or false.

Prayerfully consider the contents of the Scriptures, do not just read the Scriptures and dismiss them as just some doctrine of those who wish to impose their influence on someone else.

Study the Scriptures diligently, do not accept someone else' opinion about the Scriptures as your own, be a person of integrity, do your homework as you know you should.

Be not a puppet and dance to the tune of someone you do not know or ever heard of before, judge for yourself after much deliberation whether Jesus Christ is the Son of God or not.

Seek out those who claim to have had a personal encounter with Jesus Christ, ask questions and consider their answers prayerfully before you dismiss them as having an elusion or wishful thinking.

Thoroughly examine all of the evidence, sleep on the evidence, hasten not to a sudden decision, for in so doing you might miss an important clue that could lead you to decide that the Scriptures are right after all, to do otherwise would be unfair to yourself.

Satan is very cleaver at disguising his lies and making them to appear as being the truth, he has had a lot of practice at the art of deception, test all of his temptations against the Scriptures and if they prove false (and they will) reject them before they have a chance of leading you astray.

Sometimes his smokescreen of deception is hard to distinguish from the truth, test all he tempts you with against the word of God as found in the Holy Scriptures and then decide if he is right or wrong, being similar is not good enough, either Satan is completely right or he is complete wrong.

Satan is a master at deception, he thrives on it, his whole doctrine is based on deception, if you find even one of his claims to be false then you must declare all of his claims to be false.

Either Satan is a liar or he isn't, all of us must decide that for ourselves, no one else can make that decision for us, we are all individuals with the ability to draw our own conclusions, exercise your ability in matters like these, do not blindly follow someone else, especially Satan.

Make two columns, one under the heading of, "Satan's claims" and the other under, "Jesus' claims", now, list all of the claims of each under the appreciate column, when finished compare both columns against the Scriptures, now, who is right Jesus or Satan?

Keep an open mind when coming to your conclusions, both Jesus and Satan cannot be right, one is a liar and the other is telling the truth, make an informed decision and then live with that decision.

I wish I could make that decision for you, but I cannot. I have already made my decision and I know for a certainty that Jesus Christ is who He claims to be, the one and only begotten Son of God, Creator of the universe, Creator and sustainer of all life, Jesus is the Way, the Truth and the life, and all who come to Him shall have eternal life.

Now, it is your turn to make your decision, think long and hard, never forget that the decision that you are about to make will have a profound influence on the rest of your life and will determine where you will spend eternity.

LIKE HIM

Can it be said of you that you are truly a child of God, that you display the attributes of God by the way that you live and your manner of speech?

One can never fully display the attributes of God but one can strive in that direction and be an example for others to follow, for as long as we live in a sin filled world we will never fully achieve our goal of perfection, we will fall short in many aspects of our lives.

True perfection will only come after the death of the flesh, and then will the true man come to life and be known as a true child of God.

There was only one person who ever walked the face of this earth and was perfect, that one is the Son of God, our Lord and Master, Jesus Christ, He came from God to save sinners from the fires of hell and all who accept Jesus Christ as their personal Savior shall achieve that end.

Jesus came to pay the price for your sins and mine, this was his primary purpose for coming and living among His created beings, He came to save us from ourselves and to show us that there is a better way of life than just following the ways of the evil one, left to our own devices we would soon become lost in a morass of sin.

Though Satan may be the Prince of this world he can only do what God will allow him to do, if it were left up to Satan none of us would ever be allowed to think about or follow Jesus Christ, for Satan opposes all and any of what Jesus advocates for those who freely chose to follow Him.

Satan is on a leash and can go no further than to tempt us to follow him, though his urgings to follow him can be strong and hard to resist they can be overcome through the word of and help through the teachings of Jesus Christ, our efforts to resist Satan will be rewarded by not having to suffer the consequences of our sin.

Sin is a dead end and leads to eternal death, the ways of Jesus Christ leads to eternal life, at some point in our lives we have to make the decision as to whom we want to follow; Jesus Christ or Satan, we cannot choose the best that each has to offer and expect to have a stable life, for the two are contrary one to the other, we either cleave to the one or the other and live our lives accordingly.

To live for Satan can produce many things that can please the flesh and seem to be the right way to live, but when closely scrutinized against the word of the Holy Scriptures the things Satan wants to give us is cloaked in darkness, adversity and strife and leads only to eternal death, that which Jesus offers is out in the open and has no hidden agenda, by our own decisions we will either end up spending eternity with Jesus Christ or be cast into outer darkness separated from Jesus Christ and God forever and ever.

Many there are who start out in life with the full intention of living a righteous life, but only a few will achieve that end, it is not so important as to where we start out in life as it where we end up, at any point in our lives we can come to repentance and accept Jesus Christ as our Lord and Savior and avoid being cast from God's sight forever, but remember we know not the day of our demise so it is in our best interest to turn to Jesus Christ early in life and become as much like Him as we can with the time we have left here on earth.

Keep your eye on Jesus and the things of this world will no longer hold the luster and attraction that they held when we first came in contact with them, there are many things in this world to distract us from keeping a vigilant eye on where we want to spend eternity, but through self discipline and a desire to be free from the temptations of Satan can take us a long way on our path to eternal life with our creator and Savior, Jesus Christ, this should be the ultimate desire for all of us.

LOOK TO THE FUTURE

Let not the mistakes of the past keep you from thinking that you have no future that will amount to anything. All have made mistakes in their lives and wish that they had thought about their decisions more than they did. Taking the easy way out often leads to regret. Regret leads to despair and despair leads to self-condemnation, leaving one thinking that they are not worthy of becoming a responsible citizen of society.

Too often, we allow circumstances (sometimes beyond our control) dictate as to how we think of ourselves and our ability to becoming a responsible citizen, thus impeding our growth, whether it is physical, cultural or spiritual. In time, such thinking can lead to a lifestyle that includes disregard for the laws that govern society. Once caught in this trap it is easier to continue in it than it is to make the necessary changes in our thinking and lifestyle to become a responsible citizen of society.

Those who refuse to change more than likely will end up in prison and while there they learn from the so-called pros, thus enhancing their abilities to cheat, steal and deceive. Our prisons are full of people who think that they have been wrongly incarcerated and have done nothing wrong.

Even in prison there are opportunities to learn how to improve one's life and returning to society as a responsible citizen. Looking to the future and deciding whether one wants to continue their path of crime or change has to be decided by each individual involved. Those who refuse to change become belligerent and even if they are released from prison, they will more than likely one-day return to prison, mostly because of their hate for the laws that governs the rest of us or unresolved physiological problems.

There is however a solution to all of man's problems, whether they are mental, physical or imagined. The beginning of any solution is that the person involved has to want to change and live a more Christ-like life. This statement has to come from the heart. Change may not come as quickly as one might want and the answer to that might be to see if that person really means what they say and want for their life.

It will test one's metal (so to speak) to see if future temptations can once again take them in the wrong direction. It is a difficult and yet rewarding decision to change one's lifestyle for the good. For once under the influence of Satan, it is truly a spiritual battle more than a physical battle to overcome the bad habits of the past. With the advice obtained from the Holy Scriptures the battle to overcome Satan's temptations can be achieved and very rewarding.

The temptations themselves may linger for some period of time and in some cases for months or even years, but through perseverance, prayer and applying the truths learned from God's word to one's life will enable one to overcome whatever Satan can conjure up. To resist Satan and his temptations is by no means an easy task. Those who are overcome by his temptations often claim that an unknown voice told them to commit that particular crime, this in fact may be the truth and without the truths of God to fall back on they obey what in their heart they know is wrong.

Satan is a powerful force in this world and is often referred to as the Prince of this world. He himself is an outcast of society and does all he can to destroy the lives of all who will listen to him and follow his sadistic ways. Satan can even appear as a Shining Light and once influenced by that light he reveals his ugly self and if not properly handled one will fall victim to his evil ways and lose their proper place in the kingdom of God. Anything that does not conform to the Holy Scriptures is of Satan and has to be confronted with God's truths in order to overcome.

We are not of ourselves capable of doing battle with Satan and wining. Only through the Holy Trinity (God the Father, God the Son (Jesus Christ) and God the Holy Spirit can we be victorious over the evil in this world.

Look to the future for Jesus Christ has paid the price for our disobedience while on the cross of Calvary. He has also told us that He will return and establish His kingdom here on earth where there will be no more temptations to distract us from our spiritual journey which will culminate in our spending eternity with Him in a world where only peace (now beyond our understanding) and complete harmony will reign. This is the hope and future of all who turn to Him and live a life here on earth that is acceptable in His sight. Life here on earth is a spiritual battle, but has a reward well worth the effort. We will only realize this when we lay our earthly bodies down and awaken to the life that Jesus has prepared for all who believe in Him.

The future of all believers is far from being dim; it is brighter than the sun and holds rewards that we now know nothing about. Fight the good fight and lean on the only one who can save us from spending eternity in hell, Jesus Christ, the one and only Son of God. He loves all mankind and wants all to come to Him, but has left that decision up to every one of us. The wise one chooses eternal life over eternal damnation.

LOST SOUL

I am but a lost sinner saved by Grace, once filled with hate and shame, I wandered far and wide and enjoyed the sins I indulged in.

The shadow of death hung over me; I could not see or hear the truth that could have set me free.

Blind was I as I wandered from pillar to post, not caring whether I lived or died, it was all the same to me.

I turned from my youthful ways and lived life my way, dulled by alcohol and the desire for female companionship filled my days, the lonely hours of night I cried myself to sleep.

Helplessly and hopelessly, I wandered the road of life not knowing or caring which way I went.

Then one day from the darkness of sin, my Sunday school teachers' admonition came to mind, "You are a child of God, live life that way."

This inspired me to look as to how I was spending my life in search of the pleasures that pleased my senses rather than my soul.

This was the day that the clouds of sin began to give way to the "Light" of God and the restoration of my soul.

The struggle was long and full of potholes but today I can say, "When you are in the pit of sin look to heaven for your redemption draws nigh. God loves you and sent his Son, Jesus Christ, to redeem you from Satan's destructive hand."

LOVE IS GOD & GOD IS LOVE

The love of God is so deep and profound that man is not capable of conceiving the true meaning of the word love.

Man loves on a human basis, man loves his family and his wife, the wife loves her husband and her family, they both love their friends, but in a different way. God loves all unconditionally, man loves on the condition that his or her spouse returns the love they give.

Comparing God's love to man's love is like comparing apples and pears, they are both fruit, but of a different kind, the two are not alike and never will be.

God's love is beyond the capacity of man to fully comprehend, God's love is total love, man's love is a conditional love, you love me and I will love you.

When man's love wanes he seeks another to replace the love that he has lost, God's love is an unconditional love, a love that never wavers, never diminishes.

Man flits from one relationship to another, not really knowing what he is looking for. God's love is the same today as it was yesterday and will be the same tomorrow; God's love is permanent, never changing.

Jesus, God's one and only begotten Son came to earth out of love for mankind, not that He had to come, God did not force Jesus to come to earth, Jesus came because He loves us and wants all to live with Him forever and ever.

Love is a gift from God to man. God's love can change the life and habits of all who have the desire to change and accept Jesus Christ as their Lord and Savior. Divine love is the greatest love that man will ever know and can be enjoyed on a daily basis.

Love in patient, God is patient and waits for us to come to the realization that the only way to eternal life is through the love of Jesus Christ. His love shall endure forever and never change.

When we accept God's love and begin to demonstrate it the floodgates of God's love is opened wide and His love fills our very being and we in turn are able to love our neighbor as God loves us.

This is the awakening of man to a new life, a new way to live, and a way to reflect the love that God has bestowed upon us.

We will become as a beacon of "Light" set upon a hill for the whole world to see, a "Light" that can change the lives of all who have the desire to live a more Christ like life.

The "Light" and "Love" of God can change a life in the wink of an eye. The "Light" and "Love" of God can change a sinner into a saint and influence the lives of others around them. When we reflect such "Light" and "Love" we become as children of God.

Yes, God loves each and every one of us, regardless of who we are, where we live or the color of our skin. God looks upon the heart of man, not what he looks like or what language his speaks, God is universal.

Man can achieve God's great love through obedience, through living as God would have him live and through accepting Jesus Christ as his Savior. Man is not pure and never will be, but man can become acceptable to God through Jesus Christ and His love, then will man become fit to live with God forever and ever.

MAN DOES HAVE
A CHOICE

When we become angry with someone, we have a tendency to strike out at him or her any way that we can. One of the more common ways is verbally. What we say and how we say it is of little concern to us. We do not care about, nor are we concerned about the consequences of what we say. Verbal abuse can be just as devastating as physical abuse. It can and does make one think that they are of little value to themselves on anyone else. It can make the receiver of verbal abuse withdraw within him or herself and in some cases become suicidal. Mental treatment facilities are full of mentally disturbed people because of the results of verbal abuse.

Verbal abuse if unchecked can and does lead to more serious consequences, such as physical abuse and even murder. The perpetrator often appears to be a very loving and caring person. When anger sets in, they lose control of themselves and become as mean and hateful as Satan. Satan is the father and perpetrator of all evil, including verbal abuse, which is only one way that Satan operates.

The truth is not only are we hurting someone else through verbal abuse, but we are destroying ourselves in the process and do not even realize it. Abuse of any kind has only one result and that is the destruction of something that God has created.

After all this is what Satan wants and he will do anything, he can to achieve that end. He is like a wounded animal striking out at anyone he can before his own demise.

It takes a higher power than what we possess to cope with and finally overcome the temptations of Satan by taking the shield of truth given to us by Jesus Christ and stand behind this shield of truth while Satan takes aim at us with his fiery darts. When we take up the shield of truth Satan may increase his attack against us in hopes that we will retreat and give in to his temptations. Take your stand with the truths of God as found in the Holy Scriptures and Satan will flee from us, not because of our power, but because Satan cannot prevail over the truths of God.

Satan was once one of God's most trusted Angels until he got the idea that he wanted equal powers with God. He persuaded one third of the angels in heaven to follow him, they rose up against God, and were cast out of heaven unto earth. Satan is Prince of the air and is a powerful force here on earth, with just one agenda and that is to destroy ones belief in God, thus keeping those who follow him from achieving eternal life. The only power Satan has over anyone is the power that we ourselves give him. Satan has only the power of temptation and we have the power of truth as found in the Holy Scriptures to defeat his attempts to destroy our faith in God.

To give in to the temptations of Satan is to destroy ones relationship with God. God sent His one and only Son, Jesus Christ into this world to pay the price of the sins of the whole world and Jesus totally defeated Satan while hanging on the cross of Calvary. Satan, his fallen angels and all who fall to the temptations of Satan will be cast into the lake of fire where the worm never dies, separated from God for eternity. All who accept Jesus Christ as the Son of God and their Lord and Savior will inherit eternal life and those who follow Satan will be cast into lake of fire.

It can be and is a struggle to resist the temptations of Satan, for he has many devious ways of deceiving us that we have much to gain by following him. Like the old saying goes, "All that glitters is not gold." Satan can be very persuasive, but the results will always be the same, the destruction of self. In the end Satan cannot win, he can appear to be winning, but he and his ways are doomed. He, like those who follow him will be the cause of their own destruction.

We must think beyond this life and come to know that there are only two roads to follow in this life. One leads to self-destruction and spending eternity in the lake of fire and the other leads to God, where one will spend eternity in the new kingdom of God.

God is patient and loving and will forgive all sin, regardless of what it might be if we truly repent of our sins and turn our lives over to Him. God knows what Satan is capable of, but like the loving parent that He is He will welcome all who truly repent with open arms. There will be rejoicing in heaven when one of the lost sheep finds their way back to the Good Shepherd.

Abuse, verbal or any other kind leads to self-destruction and an unfulfilled life. God has given us the choice and authority to do with our lives, as we want. It is a great responsibility. God also gave us commonsense and the ability to make our own decisions about our own lives. He also set boundaries for us and has told us the consequences for crossing those boundaries. God is a loving and a very caring God and is concerned about each one of us.

We have choices to make and make them we must. The only time that it is too late to repent and change our ways is when we step through the door of death. Then our book of life is closed until the great Day of Judgment when it will be opened and we will be judged by its contents. It is imperative that we cast aside our evil ways while we have the chance to do so. No one is perfect, all have sinned and fallen short of the glory of God, but we can strive towards perfection and thus assure ourselves a place in God's Kingdom to come. Turn to God while there is still time and make the right choices, for ones place in eternity depends upon ones choices.

MARCHING TOWARDS ETERNITY

At the break of day, we gather at the foot of the cross and march on towards eternity. While at the cross, we leave our troubles behind and take on a new life, one fit for the kingdom of God. Once we wandered hither and yon, now we look forward to a new home, one prepared by God.

In the days of old, we sinned and did not care for we fulfilled the desires of the flesh, we were blind and could not see, and Satan held our attention and did his best to keep us from the foot of the cross.

What a change we see in our lives when we allow God to rule our lives, never to return to the days of old when we lived our lives our way, under the influence of the evil one.

When Jesus calls us home and the roll is called up yonder we can one by one answer, "Thank you Lord for fulfilling your calling while upon the cross you hung. Without Your love for us we would most certainly be lost in sin."

It is what Jesus did while hanging upon the cross that can change our lives if we turn from our wicked ways and commit our lives to the one who gave His all and paid the price for our sins.

Jesus is his name, the Son of God, the one who left His heavenly home and humbled Himself before the whole world so that the world might see beyond the cross and come to believe in Him.

Free we are who gather at the foot of the cross and submit to His will, free to pass through the pearly gates when this life is over here on earth, all others will be cast from His sight, never again to know the love that saved a wretch like you and me.

Revel in the words Jesus spoke that day while hanging upon the cross of Calvary. It was He who said, "It is finished", and He implied, "Come unto me each and every one, come to the foot of the cross and receive eternal life. It is free, come and see."

Listen and one can hear Jesus calling across the chasm of time, calling the faithful to kneel at the foot of the cross and commit their lives to him, as the scriptures say; all who come to Him shall receive eternal life.

The cross has been fulfilled, now the faithful wait for the return of Jesus and the coming of a new life and a renewed desire to serve the one who gave His life so that we might live and spend eternity with Him.

MAY MY EYES SEE AND MY EARS HEAR

As I stand before God's throne I gaze upon a sight that
no one has never known.

My eyes are closed and yet I see things that eyes have
never seen.

The brightness of His countenance lights the pathway
of man and guides him in the way that he
should go.

To describe God is not for us to do, if I open my mouth
to try my voice will not be heard.

That which I have seen makes me glow inside, but it is
not for me to describe.

It is by faith that man must accept things that are
hidden from his view.

My ears are filled with the strains of music, never
before heard by the ears of man.

To describe the tunes that I have heard cannot be done
by the likes of me, because the words of man
are too feeble and frail. The music of
heaven is beyond the ability
of man to conceive.

Let my mind be open so that I may understand the
voice that only I can hear.

My neighbors can hear it too if only they would be
still and listen and have an attentive ear.

To witness the beauty of God's throne is for all to see,
it is not just for me.

God's powers are far beyond the feeble mind of man
to understand.

May my eyes see and my mind understand that which
God has in store for me.

May I walk in God's garden of love and hear His voice
from above.

May His love fill my heart with joy and dispel the myths
that men set before me.

O Lord help me walk Thy path so straight, if I stumble
let it be in Thy hands that I tumble.

MAY YOUR WILL BE DONE IN OUR LIVES

Heavenly Father, may Your love flood our lives and through this may we feel Thy presence and may we come closer to Thee.

It is not for us to seek Thy comfort for ourselves only, but that we might conform to Thy ways and be a heavenly influence in the lives of others.

That we might learn to put self aside and witness as to how your love and concern can change lives for the better by changing how we perceive Your love towards us.

Instead of selfishly seeking things for ourselves teach us how to apply Your word to our lives, thereby bringing us into conformity with Thy will rather than expecting You to conform to our ways.

Thank You for Your patience with us as we stumble our way through this life that You have so graciously bestowed upon us, help us to realize that without You we would be lost forever in our own self centered way of life.

Guide us so that we can get beyond self and enable us to be able to reach out to our fellowman as we struggle with the conditions of life.

Teach us that the more we give of ourselves the closer we come to Thee, for only through this can we become useful to You in the advancement of Your kingdom here on earth.

May Your love be manifested through us and be an example that will help change the lives of others, not for ourselves do we seek this, but that we might be an encouragement for others to turn to Thee and allow You to become the center of their lives.

Our prayer life is at its best when we learn to put self aside and allow Your presence to fill our whole being and through this may Your "Light" shine in the darkness of sin and lead others to the foot of Your throne, there to submit themselves to Your will.

Dwell in us O Lord, use us in whatever way is pleasing to You, for this reason You created us, help us to fulfill the life that You would have us to live, for only in this way can we be any earthly good to You and our fellowman.

We seek Thy will so that others might see You through how we conduct our lives, hold us to a higher standard O Lord and when we fail Thee lift us up and renew Your love in us, for we are weak and at times become lost in our own agenda.

May Your peace and love be with us all the days of our lives and may we be an example that will encourage others to bend their knee before Thy throne and seek Thy will in their lives.

MERRILL ARTHUR PHILLIPS

My name is Merrill A. Phillips. I was born and raised in Chatham, Mass. After high school, I joined the Army Air Corp in 1944 and served during WW 11 as an aircraft mechanic. Discharge in Oct 1946 and went on to learn and work in the plumbing and heating trade.

Was married in 1949 to my first wife and we had three children. Divorced in 1962, moved to New Hampshire in 1965 where I remarried and went into business for myself in the plumbing and heating trade. This marriage lasted eight years, remarried again in 1976 and have been married for thirty-five years. We presently live in Barton, Miss., a small town in the Northwest part of the state, about eighteen miles from Memphis Tn.

God called me write in1988 while living in Arizona, two years later; I started writing and have been writing ever since. My writings are mostly inspirational, but have many sea stories and poems along with some children stories, many of which are based on personal experiences as a child. Have had some of my writings published in our local newspaper, also my church has printed one in the church bulletin each week for the last eight years. Many of my writings have been put on the internet. A church group in southern India requested permission to translate my writings into their local language and use them in their classes.

I am now eighty-five years of age and retired. I spend most of days working with my writings and still enjoy writing and putting them together in book form in hopes of some day getting them published as I can afford it.

My hope is that my writings will be of help to those who are searching for answers to life's problems or at least lead them to where they can find the answers. Without a doubt, writing has been the greatest experience of my life and have spent many hours of putting on paper what God wants me to convey to others. Without the encouragement and understanding of my wife Nell, I would not have had the time I needed to devote to my calling.

MIRACLE OF THE CROSS

One day I found myself at the foot of the cross on bended knee; I looked up and saw Jesus hanging there, with head bowed as if in prayer I heard Him say, "Father, forgive them for they not know what they do."

Then it struck me that Jesus was referring to me, for I had strayed from the way that He wanted me to live and sought the things that I thought would give me pleasure and a fulfilled life. Little did I realize that that which I sought would only bring heartache and pain.

As I kneeled there, Jesus' blood spattered on the ground, and as it did, it washed my sins away. I felt from within a surge of new life, a feeling I had never felt before, Jesus was dying and yet my life was being renewed.

From deep within I prayed this prayer; "Dear Jesus, forgive us this day for nailing You to the cross of Calvary. I understood not that you were really the Son of God and had come to earth to save a sinner such as me."

This day of days was the day that I turned my heart over to Jesus and asked Him to come into my life and make me into the person that He wanted me to be. I knew the journey would be long and yet I already felt as though I was well on my way.

At last I could hold my head high and not have to make excuses as to why I was living life my way, I had forsaken my sinful ways and declared that Jesus was my Savior and that through His sacrifice on the cross of Calvary Satan no longer had a stranglehold over me.

Jesus had opened the door to heaven and once opened it can never be close to those who come before the cross and turn their lives over to Him. Jesus, the Son of God left His heavenly home and came to earth to lay the foundation of salvation, all who surrender their lives to His will, will never have to face the trials of life alone, ever again.

Those who do not believe are blind, as blind as once was I. Blind they will be until the day that they too feel the need to come before the cross of Calvary and surrender their lives to the one who came to earth to set them free.

Once the "Light" of Jesus shines in one's life, they will always be a child of God even though they will still face the temptations that Satan uses to lure us from the path that Jesus wants us to trod.

The way may be hard and the journey long but with the sacrificial death of Jesus on the cross of Calvary one can step forth in faith and fear not what is in the way. Jesus will open the doors that need opening and close the doors of our past so that we may clearly see the path that leads to eternal life and our heavenly home.

Come hand in hand and join those who have gone on before, join in common prayer and live the new life offered by the Son of man. It is ours for the taking; it is the start of a new day, a day that has no night or shadow where sin can hide.

Jesus came to cleanse all who kneel at the foot of the cross and say, "Come into my life Lord Jesus, I am blind and cannot see the path that I should trod. Cleanse me Lord Jesus of the sins that I have committed along the way. From this day forward, I want to live life Your way and be of service to You. I am tired of my old life; renew my soul that I might say, "I belong to You.""

MIRACLES, A GIFT FROM GOD

Miracles should be viewed from the point of view that they are a natural part of life. Miracles are often looked upon as an event that cannot be explained in any other way but an event that defies explanation. Miracles are in fact events that come about through God to the benefit of man. All miracles come from God and many are answers to prayer. A spiritual healing without the intervention of man is referred to as a miracle, but in fact reflects God's love for man.

Some will try to explain miracles away by saying a miracle is no more than one exercising mind over matter, a miracle is more than that, a miracle is a gift from God. Throughout the centuries, miracles have changed the lives of many. Saul on the road to Damascus was changed in the twinkling of an eye when he encountered the "Light" of Jesus Christ. He was responsible for the persecution and death of many who were following the teachings of Jesus Christ, mainly Jews. A rogue who was out to discredit and kill all who professed the name of Jesus Christ, he was feared and hated by all who knew of his evil deeds. After his conversion, his name was changed to Paul and he went on to be the greatest evangelist the world has ever known. This is undeniably a miracle (An act of God) and at the same time, it is one of the greatest examples of how

God can change a life of criminal activity to a life of service to Him. There are many other instances where God intervened in the lives of those whom He chose to serve him in whatever capacity that He chose for them. I myself have been the recipient of such a miracle, one where my life was changed in the twinkling of an eye and have tried to be serve God in the capacity of putting on paper that which He wants me to express. I am not telling this to brag of myself but to show that even today God chooses people from each generation to serve Him.

All who diligently seek God can be the recipient of these gestures of love from God to man. Those who have received such gestures can witness to others from a first-hand point of view. They can and should tell others about what they have received from God, for one knows not who and how their experiences might influence the lives of others. If by telling ones spiritual experiences can but help just one person the effort of doing so will be well worth the effort. As the Bible teaches, one cannot hide a candle under a bushel, it has to be set on a hill where all can see and benefit from the light thereof.

Those who have been the recipient of God's grace will be the first to acknowledge that they are not someone special for in the eyes of God all are special and God's love in unconditional. When we put conditions in our thinking of how God works we are but obstructing God's ability to work through us. All doubts about how God performs His miracles have to be removed and become as an open vessel, prepared to receive with grateful hearts what God has prepared for us. No one can have a fuller life than one who serves God and does so with a willing heart. If one serves God with the anticipation of receiving monetary benefits or any other benefits is not serving God, but serving their own interests.

God is a gracious God and He and He alone deserves all the credit and honor that might come from the manifestation of His love through us towards others. Rejoice in the Lord and if you have been the recipient of His love through a miracle, then pass it on to others so that they may rejoice with you and be blessed by it. Humble yourself and become a messenger of God bearing good tidings that will benefit all. Accept miracles as an expression of God' love for man and accept that they are a part of the natural realm of our spiritual life.

MIRACLES

Miracles are a way of God expressing Himself, a way of getting our attention, a way of God saying, "Look at what I am capable of doing at any time. Marvel not at what you see, just accept it as an expression of My love for thee."

We often prefer to call miracles an unexplainable feat by God, something beyond our ability to explain, thus leaving us in wonderment as to how God can accomplish such deeds.

In reality miracles are just God's way of expressing His love for mankind, a way of showing that He has the ability to express His love through a miracle to any part of His creation at anytime regardless of what it might be.

Thinking about and accepting miracles as a gesture of God's love removes all doubt that He is in complete control of the events in the life of anyone and all who have lived or will live here on earth.

From the scriptures we conclude that God's ways are not man's ways, neither are man's ways God's ways, this is to say that God can and does express His love for us in ways that perhaps we cannot explain, ways that we must accept by faith and take into our heart and cherish for the remainder of our life.

Miracles can and often do change the lives of those who are the recipients of otherwise unexplainable events in their lives, through miracles we grow in our effort to live life as God would have us to live.

Miracles are contrary to the laws of man, thus he is at odds to explain how and why miracles take place, at times man is so blind that often he refuses to believe those who are the recipient of miracles are telling the truth.

The fact of the matter is that miracles happen every day, some may seem more spectacular than others, but they all come from the same source and are truly an expression of God's love towards mankind.

Man does not have to understand, nor will he ever fully understand how and why God chooses to use what we refer to as miracles to intercede in the lives of many, for in doing so many lives are changed for the better, leading to a better understanding of how God expresses His love towards man.

Miracles come in many and varied forms, all orchestrated by God for the betterment of those who are the recipient of miracles and for the advancement of our growth in the ways of God and most importantly to draw us closer to our creator, for God's love is so great that He will bestow miracles on those who so richly deserve them and bring about a change in their lives.

MY LORD
AND SAVIOR

Jesus Christ is my Lord and my Savior, He walks before me and tells me I am His own, He prepares me every day to face the challenges of every day life.

Jesus loves me and encourages me to be the best that I can be; He forgives me when I fall short of that goal.

He heals my body when things go wrong, He gives me the incentive to arise refreshed in the morning to go about my daily chores.

When the storm clouds of life appear He walks before me and only allows them to buffet me as I can stand, for never will He allow me to face more than I am capable of enduring.

When the rain and winds of sin cease I am stronger than before, I fall to my knees and praise Him and thank Him for sheltering me under His protective wing.

Without the Holy Trinity in my life surly I would fall prey to the evil one, for he presses me from all sides and yet God only allows him to go just so far.

With heaven' gate just around the next bend in life I fear not for God has promised that all who believe in His one and only Son, Jesus Christ, shall not die but have everlasting life and dwell with Him for eternity.

With this promise I engage each new day with the renewed hope of eternal salvation, without this hope surly my days would be filled with woe and I would become lost in the sea of sin.

God is merciful to all who turn to Him both in good times and in times of trouble, God holds the key to life and eternal life and will give it to all who bow before His throne in submission to His will.

God loves and adores all of His created beings and will guide all to eternal life If they will but let Him, thereby submit your life to God and live, live life thy way and be cast into outer darkness, separated from God for eternity.

God wants no one to be cast into outer darkness where there is no way of escaping the tortures of hell, He is willing to forgive even the most egregious offences that man can conjure up, just by putting self aside and bowing to the will of God one can enjoy all that God has in store for those who love Him.

Through Jesus Christ God created all that there is and will forgive and bless all who forsake their evil ways and turn their lives over to Him, therein lays the real riches of this life, try it and see.

MY PILOT BE

When my ship of life crosses the bar, be with me O Lord,
and my pilot be.

Guide my ship of life through the storms of life that I might
follow Thy star that leads to eternity.

As my ship of life crosses the bar O Lord my rudder be,
guide my soul on its journey to dwell with Thee.

Stand by me O Lord as my ship of life sails the open sea
and the waves of sin try to devour me.

With Thy "Light" shinning across the pages of time, light
the pathway that leads to Thy side so that my
soul might be blessed by Thee.

Blessed art though O Lord, Thy mighty wings have sheltered
me when my ship of life had been in danger of
floundering on the shoals of a sinful sea.

My pilot be O Lord I pray, guide me every step of the way,
lest I stumble and fall prey to the sin that
surrounds me day by day.

From the day of my birth to the day of my demise Thy love
encouraged me to sail my sip of life in the lee
of Thy throne.

My pilot be O Lord when my ship of life crosses the bar and
Earth I no longer can see.

MY SOUL WAS AT PEACE THE DAY MY SAVIOR CAME FOR ME

The other day as I left the old farmhouse and made my
way towards the barn my eyes fell upon yonder hill,
there I saw my Savior standing with arms
outstretched towards me.

The sky all around Him was brighter than a rising
sun, a halo outlined His head, and He
seemed to beckon to me.

With His hands raised high, I heard Him say,
"Come my son, it is time."

As I approached, I asked His blessing upon my farm. To which
He replied, "You have plowed the field and planted
the seed for many a year, now it is time to rest."

Perplexed and a little surprised I ventured to say, "Take
me in your arms O Lord and console me as this
life I leave."

With a smile on His face, my Savior took me by the hand
as we turned and walked off into eternity.

MYSTERIES

The mysteries of life are of God, for God, and by God, thus the mysteries of life are revealed through the study of God's word as found in the Holy Scriptures. What was once unknown is now known and is for the benefit of all.

We are blind to the spiritual realm and feast on the materialism of humanity, thus wandering through life with little more than a glimpse into the spiritual life. No matter how much we explore the spiritual life we never come close to experiencing the fullness of its beauty and tranquility.

The dragons of life bind us within ourselves and hinder our growth both spiritually and mentally. To conquer our dragons we battle for our sanity within ourselves encouraged by family and friends, but the main thrust of victory comes from within.

The driving force for self-fulfillment comes from what we take in and allow to influence our lives, thus we ourselves build within ourselves what we want others to see.

Though we may live within our own dungeon and reflect its character, we can escape its destructive power by opening the windows of our mind and allowing the "Light" of life to revitalize our purpose of being.

We build grand cathedrals where we express our spiritual desires and yet within those very walls we desecrate humanity with our vile thoughts and deeds. It is not the cathedral building that determines our spirituality; it is what we take in to our personal cathedral (our mind) that reflects our outlook on spirituality.

We live within ourselves and become a product of our thinking, thus we control our future by our actions of the past. Acting upon our inner feelings produces the atmosphere within which we live. To deny the power of thought is to deny the existence of a higher power. What comes from within reflects what we put first in our life and this controls our destiny.

Selecting what we take in controls our actions and how we relate to others and influence those around us. Someone is watching you and placing you in a position of honor or denying you as a lost soul.

Humility is a product of self-sacrifice and a desire to serve others without expectation of personal gain. We are a product of our own desires to serve manifested through humility. We grow through serving others and reflect the manifestation of humility as a result.

Truth is ever before us and a guide for our life, truth is a healing balm for all of life's problems whether they are of the spiritual nature or everyday events. If what we take into our hearts is to benefit others then truth has to be at its core. Truth is of God for the benefit of man, reflect that truth and triumph over sin.

NOW IS THE TIME

Come my friends from far and near, join hands in adoration for our Lord. Praise Him ye on high and ye from the depths of the valleys. Look upon His face and see the love in His eyes. Sing praises unto His name.

Return unto Him ye who have gone astray, exalt him before your fellowman. His word can heal the wounds of the nations and can bring their people to the foot of the cross. Stand fast and fear not those who seek to persecute you, but rather show love towards all. Look not unto thyself for understanding, but rather turn unto Him who created all. Fall to your knees and give thanks to whom it belongs.

Tarry not, for the hour is at hand when all shall make an account as to how they conducted their lives here on earth. Turn from sin while it is still day, for the night cometh when no man can change. This earth and all that there in is will soon pass away, stand fast in your faith and fear not the return of the Lord, but rather rejoice that he loved you enough to give his life for your sins while on the cross of Calvary.

The storm clouds gather and the sun is setting low, but His love will reign over all who stand with Him. The day that the sheep will be separated from the goats draws neigh, fall before the throne of Jesus and seek forgiveness while you may. Only Jesus

Christ holds the key to the door of salvation, He offers it to all who forsake their sinful ways and follow Him; once that door is closed, no man can open it and enter therein. Jesus refuses no one who knocks on His door and seeks his forgiveness, but knock you must if ever it is to be opened to you. We cannot pass through that door with someone else's key. Jesus knows His sheep and they know His voice and obeyeth it. Follow not his ways and be swept into oblivion, lost forever in the sea of sin.

Look not unto thy own understanding, for God's ways are not man's ways, neither are man's ways God's ways. Man cannot live by bread alone, but by every word that comes from the mouth of God and so it is that man may seek God, but will never find Him unless he submits himself to the will of God and leaves earthly things behind and puts God first in his life. The road is narrow and may be arduous that leads to eternal life, but will be well worth the effort that it takes to live a life pleasing to God.

Come ye all nations, throw your arms into the furnace and turn them into plowshares and pruning hooks, plow the fallow fields and plant them with the word of God and He in turn will water them and bring forth a righteous nation worthy of his love. His rain will fall upon the wheat and the tares, let them grow together until time of harvest and then God will separate the tares from the wheat and cast them into the eternal fires of hell.

As you travel the road of life, reach out to those in need, bind their wounds and anoint them with love. Hold not back your willingness to share the bounty that has been bestowed upon you by the Father of us all. Though we all have to work out our own salvation put no stumbling blocks in the paths of those you walk beside, encourage them, as you were encouraged.

When the hour of death surrounds you, fear not what lies ahead, for all who have followed the ways of God will awaken to a new life, free from the burdens of this world. A new home prepared for you by the Son of God, a reward for your righteousness while here on earth. Now is the time to prepare for life after death, now is the time to become a follower of Jesus Christ. Love as He has loved you, give as he has given you, so doing you will live forever in His presence.

OBEDIENCE

While working for a Baptist church many years ago I had a confrontation with the pastor and of course, I lost the argument and gave my two weeks notice, but after much thinking I realized that although my complains were legitimate I was not in control of the situation, he was. I swallowed my pride, went to his office, apologized for my actions, and continued working there. The pastor was in control of that church's business and regardless of whether he was right or not I had no right to question his authority.

Just as that preacher was in authority over that church's business so is Jesus Christ in authority over our lives and our very existence and neither do we have any right to question Jesus' authority. We are to submit to Jesus' authority and be obedient to His will for our lives. It is a hard lesson to learn to submit to another's authority especially when you believe them to be wrong. We often want to correct what we perceive as wrong and correct it to suit ourselves, but that does not make it right for us to question higher authority. Submission is a hard lesson to learn, but the sooner we learn it the more we will grow in the sight of Jesus Christ.

When disobedient we can lose our purpose in life and wander the streets of life without any purpose for living. Even though we are all disobedient at one time or another and learn lessons the hard way we can change through becoming humble and submitting to a higher authority out of respect for that authority. The results being we grow spiritually and find it easier to submit to and recognize that Jesus Christ is in authority over every aspect of our lives. Through submission, we gain respect from those in authority and in turn, they are more willing to hear what we have to say and work towards an amenable solution.

Through the years, I have done a lot of writing on many different subjects and I had to learn obedience to the calling and timing of how and when I should write. Many times, I have been awakened in the middle of the night with a subject on my mind and turned on the light and wrote for an hour or two. Other times I have been awakened with a subject on my mind and put off writing with the excuse that I would remember the subject and write about it in the morning. Come morning I had no idea or recollection of what the subject was I supposed to write about. This is to show that through obedience, we can accomplish what Jesus wants us to do, but through disobedience, He removes that subject from our minds in as much to say, "Your heart is not with me one hundred percent."

Jesus deserves one hundred percent of our attention and through obedience; we can accomplish what he wants us to do. If we cannot humble ourselves before our employers and be obedient to them then how can we humble ourselves before Jesus and be obedient to Him? Life's lessons are hard to learn when we put self in the way of obedience. Some never do submit to Jesus' calling and face the consequences of disobedience, which could be very detrimental to their future relationship with Jesus. Jesus is the potter and we are the clay, let Him mold us into the image that He wants for us through obedience and life will be easier compared to those who live life their way and face a bleak future.

ONE DAY YOU WILL BE AS I AM NOW

Why stand ye there with tears in your eyes, looking
down upon me.

I am not here; I have left your world and am now on
a new adventure with old friends as well as new.

I loved you all while I was with you, some of you
returned that love and helped me when I
was in pain.

I no longer see things as you do, for where I am all
things have become new there is no more
sorrow, heartache or pain.

The world that I now enjoy has no need of your sun
by day nor moon by night.

The "Light" thereof never grows dim, nor does it cast
any shadows where sin can hide, there is only
perfect love for all to enjoy.

My tasks are no longer burdensome to bear, they
are light and a pleasure to perform.

I now enjoy freedom that I never knew existed before,
the ever-loving arms of Jesus embrace me
as we walk and talk.

I move from place to place with the greatest of ease and
my eyes behold the beauty that abounds, my needs
are met even before I say a word. Supplied by
our heavenly Father, before
I left you behind.

As much as I loved you all, I have no desire to return to
my old ways, I just wish that you all could be
as free as I am now.

I know that that is not possible in your world, for the
sins of man stand in your way.

You will now close this box and commit my remains
to the soil from which it came.

Be not sad, but rather rejoice that I am now truly free,
free to soar with the angels and enjoy the
comforts that once eluded me.

Peace be with you all and remember that one day you
will be where I am this day.

Fear it not my friends, for there is only peace and love
in store for those of you who believe.

ONLY TWO CHOICES

It is grievous unto God when we are disobedient; as much as God loves us, He will turn His head from us and allow us to wallow in our sins. It is our choice to be disobedient, just because someone else sins is no excuse for us to sin. The inward man knows evil is wrong, but when not disciplined for our disobedience our heart becomes calloused and we lose the distinction between doing right and doing wrong. We become secure in our evil doings, think that we are invincible, and no can touch us. On judgment day, all of our deeds, evil and good will be revealed and on these, we shall be judged. There is no escaping our evil deeds. God is willing to forgive our evil deeds through repentance right up to when we pass through the door of death, but once we pass through that door of death, it is too late to repent. We have chosen our own destiny, hell.

God never intended for us to be separated from Him, it is man who separated himself from God through his evil deeds. Satan promises us wealth, power, influence over others and many other enticing ways, if only we will follow him. Satan can appear as a shinning light and convince many that his ways are right, but when examined closely and compared against the Scriptures it becomes apparent that they are evil and should be avoided at all costs. Put on the full armor of God and allow God to be our shield against the fiery darts of Satan, our knight in shining armor if you will.

Disobedience to God leads to the second death. We all shall lay down our earthly body in what we call death, but our spirit will live on and those who loved God and lived by His laws shall not know the second death. Those who chose to disobey the laws of God shall suffer the second death, separated from God for eternity. It is here in this life that we determine our place of abode when we lay our earthly body down. There is no second chance after the death of the body, it is here and now that we have a chance to repent and become a child of God, worthy of his love and the assurance of eternal life.

Just before Jesus died on the cross of Calvary He stated, "It is finished." Jesus took our sins upon himself and paid the price for them through the shedding of His blood. Satan can be compared to a bully, he can and will tempt us to stray, but once faced with the truths of the Scriptures he will flee from us. Jesus gave us permission to use His name in our fight against Satan and just the name of Jesus and Satan will back off. Satan does not have the final say, God does and nothing can change that.

The choice is yours and mine as to whom we will follow, Jesus Christ or Satan. God will honor whichever choice we make, choosing God leads to eternal life, choosing Satan leads to eternal death. Be wise in your choice. As it is written in the book of Daniel 12:10. Many shall be purified and made white, and tried. But the wicked shall do wickedly, and the wicked shall not understand, but the wise shall understand. (KJV)

Is it not better to cleave to the word of God as found in Holy Scriptures and live than it is to succumb to the temptations of Stan and die the second death, separated from God for eternity? Compare all temptations against the scriptures and if they do not agree with the scriptures then flee from them lest you fall victim to Satan's temptation and end up in hell.

OUR FINAL GOAL

O how God loves us, His love is so deep and profound that He created this universe in which we live just for you and me.

Within this world He put everything that we will ever need to sustain ourselves and our families from the beginning of time to the end of days.

Within the heart of God is the desire that all people come to Him and become one of the elect. God grieves every time one of us goes astray and loses our way.

Even then He loves us enough and awaits our awakening and our desire to return to Him as a lost sheep seeks the protection of its shepherd.

God was even reluctant to cast His beloved angel Lucifer out of heaven, but He had no choice because Lucifer rebelled against God and wanted to be equal with God. But in order to maintain a perfect place for our future abode God had no choice but to remove all disobedience from His sight.

God never tolerated disobedience from Lucifer and the angels who followed Lucifer and neither will God tolerate disobedience from His created beings, you and me.

This however did not diminish His love for us; God loves us even though we are convicted sinners in His sight.

God's love was and is so deep that He sent His one and only Son, Jesus Christ, to earth through a virgin birth to reconcile man (you and me) unto Himself.

If Jesus had come as a conquering hero man would have become obedient unto him out of fear rather than love and would have obeyed Him as a robot obeys the command of its master.

While Jesus was on earth He was in a spiritual battle with Satan (Lucifer), through quoting scripture Jesus defeated Satan at every turn.

The final battle between Jesus and Satan took place while Jesus was nailed to the cross at Calvary, it appeared that Satan was about to win, but as Jesus hung on the cross He declared "It is finished." Through this statement Jesus dealt the final blow and Satan suffered total defeat.

Jesus' shed blood was the requirement God required to negate the sins of mankind, all who repent of their sins and accept Jesus Christ as their Lord and Savior will be washed white as snow by the shed blood of Jesus Christ.

Today, Satan is a defeated foe and goes around like a roaring lion seeking whom he may devour. When Jesus returns He will cast Satan into the bottomless pit and peace shall reign for a thousand years.

Then the final disposition of Satan and his fallen angels will occur. Jesus will have to but say the word and they will cast into the lake of fire along with all who did not accept Jesus Christ as their Lord and Savior; Satan will never be a threat to mankind or anyone else ever again.

Only the righteous shall remain and they will reside with Jesus Christ forever, living in the presence of their creator. With this God's plan for mankind will be complete, peace and harmony will reign for eternity.

There will be no more sin, sorrow, sickness, disease, nor death, heavenly love will be the order of the day, and all will live in perfect harmony for ever and ever.

God's plan for mankind is so simple; obedience to God is all it takes to become a menber of His family. All who come to love God as we love and obey our earthly father will live with God for eternity; all others will suffer the second death, a death of their own making.

OUR WAY OR GOD'S WAY

As we walk through the trials of life, we either try to solve our problems our way or God's way. The results of trying to solve our problems our way often ends up making the problems worse, but when we seek advice from God we can walk in confidence if we follow His lead.

God is with us night and day, we are the one who complicates the things of life, and we know when we do wrong. We try to do things that we should take to God in prayer and wait on Him to guide us in the way that we should go.

Through the love of God, we can overcome all things. On the other hand, Satan tries to get us to ignore God and follow him, Satan's way pleases the flesh and covers up the fact that his way leads to eternal death, separation from God for eternity. God's ways leads to eternal life.

Death of the flesh separates the sheep from the goats. The sheep hears their Master's voice and obeyeth it and the Master knows every one of His sheep by name. The goats blindly follow Satan and fall into the great abyss, lost forever.

You and I have to make the decision to follow Our Lord and Master, Jesus Christ, which will require self-sacrifice and an allegiance to Jesus' teachings, which leads to eternal life, or to live life our way and become a disciple of Satan and spend eternity separated from God.

When Satan whispers, "This is the way to wealth and prosperity." or he tempts you to do wrong, listen not, rebuke him with the truths of God as found in the Holy Scriptures and he will flee from you and seek others who are unaware. To follow Satan is to walk down that dead-end road that leads to eternal death.

Jesus will never tempt us to stray; He is the one and only Son of God and in Him is no guile, just truth comes forth from His mouth, truth that we either accept by faith or reject. Jesus will never force us to do anything against our will; for we all are free agents to choose, what we perceive is best for ourselves. Unfortunately, many choose not to follow Jesus and end up spending eternity separated from God forever.

We (you and I) live either for Jesus Christ or for Satan. No one can straddle the fence and claim allegiance to both Jesus and Satan (depending on what one feels is best for them at the time.), for in reality there is no fence to straddle. Those who reject Jesus know deep within their soul that they are wrong, but for one reason or another, they do what they know to be wrong.

We all hold our final destiny in our own hands. We will reap that which we sow, how we live our lives reflects that which we believe. Jesus stands with His arms stretched heavenward calling all unto Himself. Satan stands with his hands full of that which pleases the flesh. You and I must decide whether we want self-fulfillment and self-gratification for the few years that we will live here on earth and face the danger of spending eternity in the lake of fire or whether we want to live a righteous life and spend eternity with God. The decision is yours and it is mine.

POWER IN THE BLOOD OF THE LAMB

There is power in the blood of the Lamb to heal the infirmities of man. Jesus shed His blood on the cross of Calvary so that you and I could be free from the bondage of sin. Jesus willingly gave His life so that all of mankind could have the opportunity to be cleansed from all unrighteousness.

The power of Jesus' blood to heal the infirmities of mankind is more powerful than the biggest and most powerful weapon man has ever devised. With just saying the word, Jesus could and still can heal all of man's illnesses. His word, spoken or otherwise cannot be deterred or overpowered by anything man can do or say.

It is sheer folly for man to even try to compare His power or knowledge to that of Jesus Christ and His authority as the one and only Son of God.

When Jesus ascended into heaven after His death, burial and resurrection, He sent us a comforter to take His place here on earth, which we know as the Holy Spirit. The Holy Spirit has the same attributes and healing power that Jesus has and the Holy Spirit has the same capability of doing miracles in the lives of us who live here on earth as Jesus had when He was among us.

The Holy Spirit is the third part of the Trinity, God the father, God the Son and God the Holy Spirit. As there is power in the blood of the Lamb so is there power in the word of the Holy Spirit. Throughout the ages, the power of God has been demonstrated through the Trinity and is available to heal and comfort all here on earth.

A righteous man' prayer availeth much. Through fervent prayer, anyone can call upon this power of the Trinity to heal anytime and anywhere. God hears all prayers and answers them according to His will.

The prayer of the unrighteous often goes unanswered because their heart is not right with God. One cannot go around in disregard for God and when in trouble, whether it be health wise or other wise and expect God to heal their infirmities when in their heart they deny that God is supreme over all things, great and small.

God knows the heart of every living soul here on earth and will respond to each according to that person's acceptance of His Son, Jesus Christ. This fact and this fact alone will determine where one will spend eternity when they lay their body down in death.

Those who accept Jesus Christ as the Son of God will spend eternity in the presence of God and those who reject Jesus Christ for whatever reason will be cast from God's sight into the lake of fire where their soul will be in torment for eternity. What a price to pay for one who lived their life here on earth for only what they could get out of life without regard of where they would spend eternity.

God will not be mocked or questioned as to His authority over everything here on earth or in the heavens above. God, through the Trinity gives to those who accept His Son, Jesus Christ, as their Lord and Savior and turns their life over to Him to do his will here on earth eternal life. A gift that cannot be achieved by any other means, not even good deeds. Good deeds are the results of accepting Jesus Christ as ones Lord and Savior, not a means of obtaining eternal life.

The blood of the Lamb is all-cleansing and can redeem the most violent person here on earth if they turn to God and accept His Son, Jesus Christ, as their personal Lord and Savior without reservations. They will have to accept the consequences of their behavior here on earth, but if truly repentant, they can be saved from the fires of hell.

PRAYER

The washing of the outside of the cup does not clean the inside of the cup. Man uses water to clean the outside of his body, but this does not clean the inner man. Prayer has to come from the heart of man before he can cleanse the inner man. Prayers are more than the verbal expressions of man's desires. True prayer requires that man puts self aside and allows the love of Jesus Christ and the fervent desire to do the will of God to take the place of self and self-interests. Man is to be ever mindful that not once did Jesus do His own will, but he always did the will of his Father, God.

Just before His betrayal on the Mount of Olives Jesus submitted Himself completely to his Father,'s will and in so doing He was able to endure the inquisition of the priests and His crucifixion upon the cross. He knew that He would triumph over all adversities, but between His betrayal and His triumph over death upon the cross, he had to endure the sins of mankind and only through complete faith in His Father could He so endure. Jesus' faith was faultless, thus He had the strength to overcome whatever man did to Him.

Even though Jesus is the Son of God and has of the power and wisdom of God, he is also subservient unto God. Jesus came to live with man not only to demonstrate His God given power to heal the sick and raise the dead, but also to show man the way to salvation and how man can eventually come to live in the new kingdom that he has prepared for all who come to believe in Him. Only through Jesus Christ, the Son of God can man lay claim to his rightful place in the world yet to come.

Many will come in Jesus' name and declare that only through them will they see the kingdom of God, believe them not for they are false prophets and all that they will accomplish is to lead the unsuspecting souls to and through the door of death, separated from God for eternity. Follow not the sooth talkers, their tongues speak evil, sustained by Satan with only one purpose, to deceive all unsuspecting souls they can, thus denying them their righteous place in the new world to come.

All are given the knowledge to know the difference between good and evil. Each one cultivates their belief in good or evil according as to who they put their trust in, God or Satan. Unfortunately, there are many who make the wrong choice. Greater is he who worketh in those who do good than he that worketh in those who do evil. Evil will have its day in the sun, but eventually evil will destroy its-self and will be remembered no more. Many a tyrant has risen to power and controlled through fear, but end up destroying themselves through greed and power.

All will one day humble themselves before the throne of God and fall to their knees in reverence to the King of kings and Lord of lords. Become as little children with a child like faith, for only through such a faith will anyone be granted permission to enter the kingdom of God. Prayer is the most powerful tool that we have in our struggle against evil. Prayer offers a safe haven for those who struggle in everyday life, prayer brings us closer to God, our creator. Prayer blocks out thoughts of obeying Satan and gives us a reprieve from falling victim to the wishes of Satan. Prayer enhances our ability to know God and be obedient to the word of God. Prayer can open up a new way of life, thus enabling us to live a more Christ-like life. God wants us to come to the realization that we are capable of being better than we are through obedience to his will. God wants nothing but the best for us and for us to work towards that end.

PROBLEMS OF LIFE

Most of the problems of life are not really problems until we make them problems, look at them as being a challenge, how we handle such challenges in a great part helps to determine our outlook on life.

If one is willing to have a servants attitude towards life them most if not all problems can be solved to the satisfaction of all parties involved, otherwise there will exist hard feelings and no permanent solution to any problem.

To exasperate a problem only makes things worse and can often lead to open hostilities between two factions, to work towards a mutual agreement with an open mind can turn a potential enemy into a friend.

Trying to be controlling without respect for others involved can lead to only one end, mainly the breakdown of any and all negotiations and the return to hostilities, which can only get worse with time.

History has proven time and time again that when one nation gets too envious of another nation war usually results with the loss of many lives, so is the same with individuals, somebody is going to get hurt.

The crutch of the whole matter is that there is an evil force at work in this world that most people do not realize or understand, all evil no matter what form it takes is orchestrated by Satan, for he is the prince of this world and will remain so until the second coming of Jesus Christ.

When Christ returns He will cast Satan and all of his fallen angels into the bottomless pit and seal the pit for one thousand years, during which time peace and harmony between all peoples of this world will exist.

Then will they be released only to face the final judgment and be cast into outer darkness for eternity, then and only then will peace and harmony return to the new earth forever and ever, certainly something that all Christians are looking forward to.

While evil exists on this earth it will be judged by God and He in return will meter out godly justice, for all actions both good and evil have consequences, evil for evil and good for good, this man cannot escape.

You and I have a choice to make, to follow God and reap the benefits of being a true believer or reject God and face a future in the dark recesses of hell where problems are only exasperated.

Man has the ability within himself to either solve a problem or to make it worse, listen to God and find a solution, listen to self and make it worse.

RENEWAL

Is it Thee I hear O Lord or listen I for another?

I hear a distant voice calling me and I want to go.

But stand still I will if that is what you want me to do.

I heard a voice say, "Stand still and wait, be not in a hurry to stray."

"Listen to what the Lord has to say, seek not thine own will, only His shall you obey."

"Let not the call of sin keep you from Him."

Listen not to those who say, "Come, we will have some fun, who is to know that it is sin?"

"No one can see us; no one can hear, let's do it before the light of day."

When the dawn breaks the sin will be hard to bear, it will weigh you down and keep you from seeing His ways.

Eventually sin will keep you from Him and you will hear Him say, "Sorry, you chose sin when you strayed, now I must throw you away."

Be not one of those who lost their way, repent and you will hear Him say, "Welcome back to the fold, I have washed your sins away."

RETURN
TO PARADISE

Satan enticed Eve to partake of the fruit of the forbidden tree of good and evil and she became the first to know evil. Before she ate of the fruit of this tree, she like Adam was aware of God only. Eve in turn enticed Adam to eat of the same fruit and he too became aware of evil. Upon gaining this knowledge, they both became aware of their nakedness and felt shame. They used fig leaves to cover themselves and as hard as they tried, they could not hide from God.

God in all of His wisdom cast them both out the Garden of Eden before they ate of the tree of life. Time and time again, God sent His messengers with the message of repentance and man ignored the warnings and kept on sinning. Then God sent His only Son, Jesus Christ, into the world to set the example for man to follow and to open the door to eternal life to all who would give up their sinful ways and follow Him, but man killed the Son of God on the cross of Calvary and thought that he was rid of Him. Thus setting themselves up for the fall.

Satan has set up many stumbling blocks in man's journey back to paradise and many there are who fall by the wayside, lost forever, never to feel the love of God again, but rather His wrath. As it is written, narrow is the way that leads to Paradise and few there are who finish the race. When man looks at life as being the only means by which he can learn about God and his love and what he has to do in order to return to Paradise then he becomes serious about following Jesus. Jesus tells us, "I am the way, the truth and the life, those who believe in me shall never die, but have eternal life." Thus proclaiming that He (Jesus) holds the key to eternal life and that He will give that key to all who forsake their evil ways and follow Him.

The lusts of the flesh and the promises of Satan for wealth, power, and self-fulfillment can be very hard to ignore, especially if one is in dire straits and is struggling with every-day life. The easy way out entraps many, at first it seems right for they can see the end to their troubles, but as time passes they find themselves in a life of crime. If they harden their heart and stay with that kind of lifestyle, they become lost without hope of changing their ways. Satan can disguise himself as a shining light and lead many to jump off the cliff and perish in their own sins. Sometimes it may be hard to distinguish between right and wrong, but when something that seems right is tested against the scriptures, the scriptures will reveal its true worth.

The road to overcoming sin is full of potholes and makes the journey towards salvation bumpy and hazardous, for Satan hates to give up in his quest to destroy man through sin. However, those who keep their eyes on the final goal will and can overcome the hazardous journey and reap the rewards of their efforts, eternal life.

It is never folly to turn to Jesus Christ when in need, He will guide the seeking heart in the way that he should go and supply his every need in order to overcome the wiles of Satan. Satan destroys; Jesus saves that which is lost. Jesus is the only way to eternal life and all who call upon His name shall not be turned away, but rather they will be filled with the Holy Spirit and become as a light set upon a hill, an example for others to follow.

This earthly journey is but as a training ground for that which is to come. Depending on which road one takes as to where they will spend eternity. Though we were conceived and born in sin, we need not fall victim to sin. In John 3:16 it is clear that we have an advocate with God who will stand up for those who choose to follow the path of righteousness.

John 3:16
For God so loved the world, that he gave his only begotten Son, that whosoever believeth in him should not perish, but have everlasting life.

SATAN

Speaketh no evil nor let it dwell in your heart lest it break forth and consume you, Satan is sadistic and cares not if you believe or not, he will do his best to compel you to submit to his will.

Those who know this and are aware of his sadistic ways turn to Jesus, so that in Him and through Him they can confront the evil proposals put forth by Satan.

Even a child of God is not exempt from the temptations of Satan for as long as one lives in this sin filled world they will be bombarded with Satan' never ending endeavors of temptation.

Keepest thou heart pure and full of the word of God and Satan will be powerless against you, he cannot distort the truths as set forth in the pages of the Holy Scriptures.

Through the Holy Scriptures one can find relief and need not bow before the throne of perdition, for once Satan is faced with the truth he will flee from you and seek weaker prey, he does not have the fortitude to do otherwise.

However Satan will from time to time come against you in the same way and try once again to entice you to be obedient to him, but re-invoking the truths as found in the Holy Scriptures and he will leave thee.

As the sun rises every morning indulge in the word of God and store it in your heart and on many occasions Satan will pass you by knowing that you are well equipped to resist him and have a place of refuge in the Holy Scriptures.

As long as we reside on this earth Satan will in one way or another test us to see if he can find a chink in our armor and catch us off guard.

Devious in his ways is he but also he is subject to the will of God just like you and I, for God is in complete control of all things, even when it seems as though He has lost control of the situation God is in control, He will often allow things to happen even though we may not understand why.

God has given man a free will to live life as he wants and if man falls to the temptations of Satan God will not interfere in our decisions until we ourselves give Him permission to do so, this is accomplished by us turning to God and asking Him to intervene on our behalf, but even then we will more than likely have to suffer the consequences of our sins.

We of ourselves do not have the power or strength to resist Satan' overtures on our own, it is only when we invoke the truths of God and call upon Him to fight our battles against evil for us that we can triumph over evil, we can of ourselves do nothing but through God we can do all things.

Do not try to fight the battle alone, we can never win by ourselves, the battle belongs to God, turn to Him and let God do it for you and when the battle is won bow before the throne of God in submission and gratitude, remember this; Satan is under the jurisdiction of God and can in no wise force us to obey him without our permission, as God cannot force His will on us neither can Satan.

SAVED BY GRACE

Once I was blind and could not see that the wickedness I
indulged in kept me in the darkness of sin.

Sin fulfilled my earthly desires and promised me prestige, a
life without cares, coins in my pocket and control over
those beneath me.

Where else could I go to have my desirers fulfilled, Satan had
me under his spell, enticing me to stray and doubt
the love God had for me.

I lost interest in the things of faith, those who believed lived a
life unbecoming to me, one filled with sacrifice and
pain, at least that is the way it seemed to me.

I had fallen from grace and looked not for a way to return to
the childhood faith that my Sunday school teacher
had instilled in me.

In despair I clung to my sinful ways, then one day I fell to my
knees and bowed my head in prayer, seeking a way
to free myself from my sinful ways.

I looked heavenward and there I saw the Lord's shinning face
looking down at me, with eyes filled with love He
reached out and touched my soul.

He stirred within a desire to change my ways and serve Him,
I felt renewed as I bowed before His throne, thankful that
He had extended His hand to me in my time of need.

Peace now prevails where once I had wrestled with the calling of the one who could save my soul from the fires of hell and as I sought to fulfill the desires of the flesh.

My soul rejoices as I espouse to others of how God reached down from heaven that day and saved a wretch like me.

SEEK GOD WHILE YOU CAN

Praise Him, praise Him O my soul, go before His throne and adore him, for He is the keeper of thy soul.

When the troubles of this world overwhelm you go before the throne of God and leave your struggles there and He will comfort your soul.

Call upon the Son of God, Jesus Christ, and He will enlighten your days here on earth, He will guide you through the trials of life when you surrender to His will.

Praise Him night and day O my soul, seek His solace when the shadow of sin enshrouds you and tempts you to stray.

God's love for you is greater than that which is in the world; it is never failing, always there, night or day.

When Jesus Christ left this world, He sent us a comforter, he is the Holy Spirit, the third part of the Trinity and through Him, we can draw close to God and His ever-loving hand.

Praise Father, Son, and Holy Spirit, praise them day and night, as you walk your road of life and the clouds of sin will pass you by.

Even Satan cannot go beyond his bounds, for he is on a leash and can only go and do what God, the Father of all will allow, temptation is his game and that is all.

Turn to God the Father, God the Son, and God the Holy Spirit when tempted to stray, with love they will strengthen you and give you victory over the temptations of this sin-filled world.

Now is the time to turn your life over to divine guidance, for one knows not the day of their demise, praise God as you traverse this life and fear not tomorrow, for tomorrow will soon be yesterday and all will be well.

Praise God O my soul, for where God resides evil cannot survive, now is the day of thy salvation and all will be well with thy soul.

When the body is laid to rest thy soul will rise to heavenly heights and forevermore be with the Lord, praise the Lord in thy last days and fear not death, for death is like a fleeting cloud, when it passes thy soul will be embraced by the "Light" of God and there dwell forevermore.

SEEKING TO LIVE
A MORE CHRIST
LIKE LIFE

No matter how much we read the Bible and try to apply the word of God to our lives we will fall short of perfection and in our efforts to emulate the teachings of Jesus Christ we will fail. We live in a sin-filled world and are bombarded by the temptations of Satan every day of our lives. Whether it is by open rebellion against God or just subtle ways of ignoring the teachings of the Bible, in one way or the other we will fall short of perfection. Even the most devout follower of Jesus Christ will never achieve perfection. We can only strive for perfection through His teachings by applying them to our lives.

As we grow in the knowledge and grace of Jesus Christ, we come to see beyond ourselves and reach out to our brothers and sisters who are searching for the same things we are and help them on their journey of life and in the process helping ourselves in what it means to be our brother's keeper. In this process, we dispel the old adage that once the apple has started to rot it cannot be saved. Just as one cuts out the bad part of the apple and discards it so can we dispose of old habits and replace them with the love and truth of Jesus that can heal the wounds of sin. There may be scars left, but they will serve as a reminder that Jesus is our redeemer and friend who loved us enough to sacrifice His life on the cross in payment for our sins so that we can achieve eternal life and through eternal life achieve perfection.

Jesus' redemptive love transcends time and is just effective today as when He was here on earth over two thousand years ago. Jesus Christ is the door to eternal life and no matter who or how many claim to have the secret to eternal life and perfection have no truth in them and are representatives of Satan, trying to deceive even the elect. For a period of time they may be effective in their efforts through deceit but once exposed to the truths of God, they are exposed as being like ravaging wolves trying to fill their own pockets. They espouse half-truths that lead many astray. It is imperative to expose all teachings to the truths as found in the Holy Bible and if found to be sound then follow them, otherwise cast them away before you become enticed to follow them and end up a victim of Satan.

Jesus knocks on our door of life, some hear and open the door and asks Him to come into their lives, thus avoiding much of the deception that many offer in the name of Jesus. Others ignore Jesus and listen to those who espouse enough of the truth to make them sound as though they are worthy of following. Words and suggestions when put in the right light can deceive many and lead them down the path of destruction. It is for each one to either receive the word of Jesus and adhere to it and live a life more pleasing to God or reject Jesus' admonitions and put ourselves in danger of the damnation.

Extend your hand to your brothers and sisters in Christ' love as Jesus extended his hand to you, share the love of Jesus and how it has changed your life and your perception of others. We are all children of God living life in many different ways with but one purpose in mind, seeking to live life in the light of God's word. Life's experiences molds our thinking and either brings us closer to God or drives us away, that is why it is our obligation as Christians to live a life that others may see God in how we live and want the same for themselves. We are to be as a "Light" set upon a hill, reflecting God's love in our lives, a love that is all-inclusive and at the same time does not put one above another, for all are equal in the sight of God.

SELF IMPOSED STUMBLING BLOCKS

Self-imposed stumbling blocks can and often do interfere with our prayer life. We pray for deliverance from both physical problems and social problems, but when we put obstacles in the way of fervent prayer our prayers are as smoke in the wind. Holding a grudge or wishing others harm for what they have done to us, I deserve an answer, God does not care about me and other such stumbling blocks do prevent us from having a good prayer life.

Un-forgiveness is also a stumbling block to a satisfactory prayer life, for while we hold hostile feelings towards our neighbor we are as much as telling God to punish those who violate our sense of right and wrong, rather than seeking forgiveness for our own shortcomings. While we harbor hard feelings against others, we are also blocking our own channel of communication with God. Seek forgiveness for our own sins and then ask God to bless our adversaries rather than to punish them for their sins. We all have sins enough of our own without trying to manipulate God into doing what is against His nature.

It has to be a two way street, clear of all obstacles in order for there to be a free flow of prayer to God and a clear path to receive answers to our prayers. Hate and love cannot coexist. God does not love us one minute and hate us the next, God loves us all the same, all of the time and waits for us to turn to Him for forgiveness. As we forgive so are we forgiven, forgiving does not mean to forgive for the moment or until we get what we want, true forgiveness means that we remember no more what others have done unto us and treat them as a true friend. Then can a meaningful prayer life exist. As Jesus told Saul on the road to Damascus (Acts: 9:5 in part) it is hard for thee to kick against the pricks. Not the pricks of a bramble bush, but rather they represent the stumbling blocks that man puts between himself and God.

Through removing the stumbling blocks, we free ourselves of our self-imposed burdens. Burdens that will hold us back and keep us from receiving answers to our prayers. Stumbling blocks can be compared to the suns inability to shine through the clouds and warm the earth. Only when the clouds pass can the sunlight warm the earth and be a benefit to mankind. So it is with stumbling blocks, as long as they exist they prevent us from enjoying a good relationship with God and our fellow man. Seek freedom from stumbling blocks while there is still time and enjoy the true freedom that comes when we remove our self-imposed stumbling blocks.

STAND GUARD

After boarding an airplane at Logan airport in Boston on my way home from a visit with my son and his family, I overheard a conversation between a Nun and one of her charges. He was one of about twelve young people who had physical handicaps of one kind or another and had been in Boston on a sightseeing trip. This young man apparently had a weakness for sweets and while in the airport terminal, he had bought and eaten as much candy as he could before the Nun caught him. The Nun had restrained him as much as she could and was telling him about the bad effects that too much candy could have on the health of his body. He was listening to what she was telling him but at the same time trying to stuff more candy into his mouth. One of her statements to this young man was, "Whatever you put into your mouth becomes a part of you."

No truer word have ever been spoken, no matter what we put into our mouths, does in fact become a part of us and can and does affect the health of our body. The Nun went on to explain that too much candy or sweets of any kind can be detrimental to our health and should be limited. She had his best interests at heart and he in return put the rest of the candy in his pocket and took his seat.

It is the same with our spiritual life; we have to watch what we read, whom we listen to and what we come to believe. Many charlatans in this world proclaim that they have special knowledge that no one else has and encourage people to believe their rhetoric and support them financially. Those who fall victim to these charlatans are taking in false doctrine and building their spiritual life on quicksand that when put to the test will fail them. Only that which is verifiable through the Holy Scriptures is appropriate to form the foundation to one's spiritual life.

The entertainment media of today is so extensive and based many times on criminal activity that is constantly bombarding the minds of our youth with the idea that crime does in fact have rewards. Monetary rewards that can fill one's pockets with more money than they can make at a menial job, thus encouraging them to join gangs and lead a life of crime. TV in notorious in the crime programs that they present to the public, every day and night crime programs instill the skills of crime in the minds of those who gravitate towards that kind of lifestyle. Even though these stories show the criminal, being apprehended they have already done their damage in the minds of the young viewers. They reason that if they commit the same crime in just a little different manner they may get away with it. Law enforcement officers work tirelessly in their efforts to curb crime, at times they become overwhelmed by the never-ending senseless crimes and killings on our streets and in our neighborhoods. This is a prime example of what one takes in directly affects how they work and live.

Solutions to the crime problem are not that hard to find and may not be that easy to implement, but the Bible has a solution for combating crime.

Through the Bible and the family unit, crime or most of the criminal activities can be curtailed and turned around. The breakdown of the family unit is the biggest contributor to the enhancement of the criminal activities that we see today. The restoration of the family unit will go a long way in reversing criminal activities in our society. In the Bible, one can find all kinds of criminal activities; the punishments for these activities are also disclosed. The ultimate punishment for crime comes when the offender stands before the judgment seat of God and hears God refuse them entry into the kingdom of God and banishes them to hell. We condemn ourselves to hell through our un-repented sins, which includes criminal activities. This and this alone should encourage one to reconsider a life of crime, for nothing can be hidden from God and all will have to account for how they lived their life here on earth. This may sound like a simplistic approach to our crime problem but this approach is one that will work.

The saying, "There are none so blind as those who do not want to see." applies to all in reference as to what they allow themselves to be influenced by, whether it be secular or spiritual. Each one is responsible for what they allow to enter their lives and or their body, whether it is too much sweets or the inculcation to live a life unbecoming an up-right citizen. Self-discipline can curb one's appetite for the things that offer rewards without having to work for them. It is better to live a life in poverty and be a friend to your fellowman than it is to live a life always looking over your shoulder to see if someone saw you commit a crime against society. Stand guard over what the world has to offer and only allow that which is good to enter into your life. Just as too many sweets can be harmful to your health, so can what you allow to enter your life control how you live.

STRANGERS IN
A STRANGE LAND

We are all strangers in a strange land, surrounded by
sin that tries to take us in.

With the wave of the hand or nod of the head we in-
dulge in the pleasures of sin.

Without thought of our future, we fulfill the whims
of our mind.

Throwing caution aside, we walk on the wrong side.

Not until we fall to the bottom of the pit can we look
up and change our mind.

Too many tempting things keep us from our Father's
side.

When in youth we cannot see the wrong in following
the crowd until we stumble and fall.

As we grow in the word of the Lord, we put childish
things aside and strive to live a life pleasing
to Him.

Being sinners all we find it hard to turn from our
sinful ways and take up our cross and walk
by our Master's side.

STRING OF LOVE

The string of love contains many different threads, some of are:

The thread of forgiveness;
We, through the love of God are able to forgive all of the transgressions against us, regardless of their origin.

The thread of compassion;
We are to look upon our fellowman as an equal and reach out to him in his time of need with love and whatever else it will take to help him through his trying times. This in turn will be passed on to others and thus spreads to encompass all of mankind.

The thread of willingness;
The willingness to help others without thought of self. If you have the means with which to help, others do it willingly and by so doing lay up treasures in heaven.

The thread of cheerfulness;
We are called to look on the bright side and not dwell on the gloom and doom things of this life. It is better to have a cheerful outlook on life than it is to go around dwelling on the gloom and doom, for that only leads to self-pity, which can affect all aspects of one's life.

The thread of witnessing;

Spread the word of God. Tell others the good news of the Scriptures whenever the opportunity arises. Give your personal testimony, as it may be just what someone else needs to hear.

The thread of truth;
Speak the truth. Do not try to deceive, for it may just come to haunt you later on in life. In the end, truth shall prevail. The scriptures tell us that the truth will set us free, free to live a life pleasing to God.

The thread of being your brother's keeper;
If your brother is in need and you have, the ability to supply that need then supply it with a cheerful heart. Expect nothing in return. Jesus gave His life for you and me on the cross of Calvary so that we can be free from the bondage of sin. No greater example of being your brother's keeper has ever taken place.

These threads and many others are all intertwined and wrapped with the greatest thread of all. The thread of love, the love that God has for all of mankind.

Jesus Christ throws us this string of love and it is up to each of us as to whether we hold fast to this string of love or whether we let go of it and sink into the darkness of the abyss, from which we will never return.

I encourage all to grab hold of the string of love and hold fast, for it feeds and nourishes our soul. It is like a life preserver that can keep us from drowning in sin.

This string of love is like a supporting handrail on our pathway of life. A pathway that leads to the foot of the cross and eternity in the presence our Lord and Master, Jesus Christ.

SURRENDER

To say, "Jesus, I love you." is to say, "I want what You have to offer, teach me Your ways." This statement is in fact a declaration of surrender to a way of life that leads to eternal life.

While others are going around seeking things that pleases the senses, you are willing to give your services to the advancement of God's kingdom here on earth.

Life is short and our days on earth are as clouds in the sky, ever changing, visible for a short while then gone forever.

Sometimes life is pleasant like cotton-puff clouds scudding across an azure sky, other times life is like storm clouds full of violent weather, destructive in nature.

In a way becoming more like Jesus Christ is like the changing clouds, sometimes the going is pleasant like puffy white clouds, other times following Jesus we run into many storm clouds and obstacles that try to keep us from achieving our goal.

The trials and fires that we are called to go through are indeed in our best interests, for they burn away the dross and we become more like pure gold, gold that is fit to put into the treasure chest of God.

It may mean giving up our lifelong ambition of becoming independently wealthy or some prestigious accomplishment, these are all well and good goals, but they in themselves cannot lead us to eternal life with God.

The person who lives life for and through Jesus Christ with little if any material wealth will enter into the kingdom of God before the one who has put materialism and the pursuit of wealth and power before their spiritual endeavors.

God does not promise wealth and materialism for us, but He does promise that those who forsake the ways of the world and accept His Son, Jesus Christ, as their Lord and Savior and live life according to His word shall inherit eternal life and live with Him for eternity.

This process does require us to walk the straight and narrow path, take up our cross, and follow Jesus and be willing to give our lives for His cause when confronted with the decision of who we are to obey, Satan of Jesus.

If Satan had his way, no one would achieve eternal life with Jesus, but that all would be condemned to the pits of hell. For it is Satan's desire and ambition to destroy all of God's creation that he can before he himself is cast into the lake of fire forever and ever and where he will never again have any power over anyone.

Even now, Satan's power is limited and he can only tempt us to obey him. Satan is on a leash, he can only go so far, and no further, therefore he can only do what God will allow him to do. Resist the temptations of Satan through the word of God and he will flee from you, for he cannot control us without our permission.

Jesus Christ is not against materialism, what He is against is when we put materialism before Him, this is when we become lost and lose sight of our intended goal of spending eternity with Jesus, a very dangerous place to be and one if not corrected before death will result in being cast from God's sight for eternity.

Those who choose to follow Jesus Christ will lack for nothing, for Jesus will supply all of their needs, not all of their wants. No one has gone without the necessities of life when they follow Jesus, He knows our needs before we do and will supply them to those who put Him first in their lives.

Materialism in not the answer to having a fulfilled life, for materialism is here today and gone tomorrow, whereas the love of Jesus Christ is the same today as it was yesterday and will be the same tomorrow. Jesus never changes, on the other hand Satan and his offerings change from moment to moment.

Surrender to the will of God and live forever, succumb to the temptations of Satan and face eternity separated from God forever. Life is a process of choices; choose well for the day will come when our choices will determine where we will spend eternity.

THE BOOK OF LIFE
HOLY BIBLE

H—How is your relationship with Jesus Christ?

O—Only through Jesus Christ can we have eternal life.

L—Leaving eternal life to chance is condemning oneself to hell.

Y—You are the only one who can save yourself from going to hell by accepting Jesus Christ as your Lord and Savior.

B—Before it is too late turn from your wicked ways and ask forgiveness from Jesus Christ and turn your life over to Him.

I—It is never too late to seek our Lord and Savior Jesus Christ.

B—Be vigilant in your quest for a relationship with Jesus Christ, He invites all to come to Him and be saved.

L—Live your life in compliance with the Bible teachings and inherit eternal Life.

E—Every day we have a new opportunity to spread the truths of the Bible to those we meet as we go about our daily lives.

THE CROSS IS EMPTY

Though Jesus died on a Roman cross over two thousand years ago, yet He lives, for the cross was just a means by which Jesus left this world to return to His Father's side.

You and I must one day die to the flesh in order to be raised up in an incorruptible body; Jesus showed us the way, for He is the way, the truth, and the life, as He lives so shall we.

For many the cross is a symbol of death, for the Christian the cross is a symbol of life beyond death, a life Christians look forward to, for to spend eternity with our Lord and Savior, Jesus Christ, death has to be endured, except in the case if we are alive when Jesus returns.

To leave family and friends behind brings sorrow to all, for a Christian looking beyond the grave brings joy to the heart, for Jesus awaits all who claim Him as their Lord and Savior, those who reject Jesus regard death as not only the end of life but that the body never really existed in the first place, (more like life is only an illusion.)

When the fruit of a tree falls to the ground it rots and is no more, but the seed of that fruit sprouts and grows a new tree, so it is with the death of the body, the body decays and returns to the soil from which is was formed, but the spirit goes on to live either with Jesus Christ or cast into the fires of hell, depending upon ones choices while living here on earth.

Jesus' death and resurrection proved beyond a doubt that there is life beyond the grave and that it is available to all just by accepting Jesus as the one and only Son of God and after that living a life reflecting that belief.

Satan reflects the dark side of life; he is without a doubt responsible for thousands upon thousands of people who live life their way, in utter disregard of the consequences of living an unrighteous life.

Satan is very deceptive and even the most ardent Christian cannot take Satan lightly, although Satan cannot force anyone to believe in him or follow him, he does have the ability to tempt us to do so, he also can try to impress upon us that he can not control our actions, but faced with the truths as found in the Bible he will flee from us and seek others whom he may destroy.

Satan knows the Bible better than we know it and often times uses scripture to try and deceive us and lead us astray, at this he is very good, he may be the prince of this world, but his powers are limited and beyond them he cannot go, he is like a mad dog on a lease, he can go just so far and no further.

Jesus totally defeated Satan and his fallen angels as He shed His blood on the cross at Calvary, for Jesus so loved all of mankind that He gave His life as an acceptable sacrifice for the sins of the whole world,

Satan is still active in the lives of all of us, but he knows that his time is limited and that one day he too will be cast into the fires of hell, there suffer the consequences of his rebellion against God forever and ever.

Yes, the cross is empty, but the one who gave His life upon that cross for you and me lives forever and forever will be our Lord and Savior, Jesus Christ is His name, He calls all to repentance. Have you answered His call?

THE FETUS HAS LIFE

If you have ever seen a TV program about the unborn child or seen a sonogram, it clearly shows that there is life before birth. The unborn fetus not only moves, but it shows the fetus putting its thumb into its mouth, moving its arms and legs around. It is clearly shows movement of life, not just a blob to be torn limb from limb and thrown in the trash just because the mother does not want it. The fetus is a living soul just like you and I, capable of independent movement. It is a living person, its heart beats, its blood circulates throughout its circulatory system, and it takes nourishment provided by its mother.

How a mature, well-educated, well-informed doctor or anyone else can kill a living, soul is incomprehensible. True the fetus depends upon the mother to survive until it is developed enough to survive on its own, it is also true that it could not survive on its own if it were taken from its mother before it was ready, but this is no excuse for interrupting that process. To do so is murder and no matter what argument the doctor or mother might make in favoring an abortion it is still murder and they will at one time or another pay the consequence for such a decision.

God is the one who gave us life and He and He alone is the only one who has the right to end it. Those who advocate abortion and perform abortions are playing god and putting themselves in danger of the damnation. It is a tragic mistake to take a life through abortion, not only is the fetus denied life but many times the mother pays the ultimate price of death due to a botched abortion. Over the years millions of fetuses have been aborted, thus, generations of people have been denied life and the pleasures of life that we take for granted. What if your mother decided to have an abortion instead of bring you to full term?

Abortion is a tool of Satan and he wrings his hands in joy when a doctor takes the life of the unborn. He clouds their mind and hides the truth from them, but one day they will face Jesus Christ and have to explain why they did the dastardly deed of taking a human life. All who set themselves above the laws of God and think that they are immured from His laws are sadly mistaken and will be held responsible for their actions, God's way.

Life begins at conception and no matter what argument anyone makes to the contrary, it is the way that it is and cannot be changed just because someone has the mistaken idea that the unborn do not have the same rights and privileges as the rest of us. Without conception, pregnancy, and birth their wouldn't be a human race, so who are we to interfere with or change the way that God chose to populate this world? Life is a gift from God.

It is Satan who deceives and prods man to turn against his creator and makes evil seem right. Satan is behind the idea that life can be taken through abortion, just as he is the root of all evil. Turn from Satan and seek God while there is still time. God knew us before we were in our mother's womb. Live by the laws of God and acknowledge that there is life at conception and that that life is precious in the sight of God and the fetus is to be honored by allowing it to come to full term.

THE GREAT GARDENER

Before a gardener plants his flowers or vegetables, he prepares the ground by spading it up and removing the unwanted vegetation and whatever else might interfere with the growth of the seedlings. After removing the new seedlings from their pot and planting them, he waters them to settle the soil around their roots; he further nurtures them as necessary to ensure their growth. He will dote over them and protect them from invading insects. When properly cared for the seedlings will grow to maturity and produce beautiful flowers or wholesome vegetables.

So it is with man, God will allow us to lose our earthly treasures, sometimes through divorce, accident, or whatever other means it will take to put us in a position where we have to make a choice to turn to God for help or continue in our downward spiral. God will not put anymore on us than we can endure, but there are some who cannot stand the strain of the situation and turn to ways that are not compatible with the plans that God has for those whom He is preparing to serve Him. Some fall by the wayside, while others endure and come to be of service to God and fill the place He has prepared for them.

While making the transition and rebuilding of their life they will be encouraged to conform to the will of God and be planted in a new seedbed previously prepared by God. God will water them with His word as found in the Holy Scriptures and as their roots grow in their new seedbed, they become more confident that they will have a brighter future. Not understanding why they had to go through this process of being replanted they go about life as usual, not fully realizing that they are being changed. This can be an arduous journey and a time to reflect on the past events and what the future might hold.

As the gardener goes to great lengths to prepare his vegetable or flower bed and the planting of the various seeds or plants and waters them to ensure their growth, so does God go to great lengths to prepare those whom He has chosen to serve Him. When the time is right God will make it perfectly clear to those whom He has chosen to serve Him just what it is that He wants them to do. Somewhat bewildered perhaps, the chosen make excuses as to why they are not qualified to step forward and serve God. Until they submit to the calling of God, God will nudge them now and again until they either submit to their calling or run the other way. God will not force anyone to follow Him, but He will force him or her to say yes or no.

To be a willing tool in the hands of God is without a doubt the greatest adventure anyone could embark on and the most rewarding. A humbling experience that can only be compared to the greatest thrill of one's life, nothing can take its place. It is not a calling that will ensure great prestige or wealth, for many who serve God live a simple life, many times unnoticed by the general public. Inwardly it does promise eternal life, eternal life that cannot be bought at any price, a free gift from God for those who choose to serve Him. This gift is also extended to those who accept Jesus Christ as their Lord and Savior.

God calls many to serve him, but few there are who answer that calling. To serve God is to deny thyself the riches of the world and depend upon God for every need. He who serves God without expectation shall receive their reward in heaven. Through God's love, all things are possible and can be achieved through submission to the one who created us, God. When called to serve God prepare thyself for the greatest journey of your live, nothing can compare to knowing that you serve God the creator of the universe and all that therein is. God in His infinite wisdom will bless and keep those who choose to serve Him.

Romans 8:28, And we know that all things work together for good to them that love God, to them who are the called according to his purpose.

Romans 8:30-31, Moreover whom he did predestinate, them he also called: and whom he called, them he also justified: and whom he justified, them he also glorified. What shall we then say to these things? If God be for us, who can be against us?

THE MAN ON THE HILL

He seemed like any other man, He ate, He slept when he was tired, and He moved from place to place as many of us do, He worked to pay his own way and yet there was something special about him. He never complained, He never condemned anyone and He was a friend to all. He taught the ways of love, and He preached his Father's word. He had power to heal the sick and the maimed. When it came time for him to leave this world, He never once opposed the verdict that was imposed upon him. He only asked his Father to give him the strength to endure that which He had to face. Never once did He raise his hand in violence against his fellowman, nor did He curse those who sought to do him harm. He endured the ridicule of those in high places. His only desire was to do his Father's will and do it with dignity and pride.

He allowed himself to be nailed to a cross like any other debtor of his time. The nails that pierced his flesh were in reality your sins and mine. Like the man that He was, He took our sins upon himself and bore their pain. He was more than willing to die for your sins and mine.

Never once did He hesitate to express his love for us, not even as He hung on the cross. While upon that cross, He was ridiculed and scorned and yet He asked his Father to forgive us for we knew not what we were doing. We crucified the one and only man who could save us from ourselves and not until it was all over did we understand that which we had done.

There are those yet who do not believe that He was who he claimed to be. Many there are who still deny Jesus Christ and that He is the Son of God. These like their counter parts of long ago are still wandering through this life with no compass (Jesus Christ) to guide them. It is only when they come face to face with the past will they realize what a mistake they have made. Only then will they try to make amends for their sin of putting Jesus to death on that cross.

Man is weak, Jesus knows this, and this is one reason that his love has transcended the ages and still embraces all who seek his loving forgiveness. Seek not your own will, but rather seek the will of the one who died for our sins upon that cross long ago and yet it seems like only yesterday that He shed his blood for all of mankind.

Though we are weak that man upon that cross will give us the strength to endure all things and never will he put more on us than we can endure. The "Light" that emanates from his very soul encompasses all who seek to do his will and repent of their sins. Like men of all times, we cannot survive without His love and His "Light" to light the pathway that we are asked to trod.

Looking back, we cannot change that which was done to that man on the hill, but we can change ourselves so that tomorrow we will be able to join Him in paradise and live under the umbrella of His love, free from this burdensome world and all of its sin. Pray therefore that Jesus will soon return and lift all worthy souls to a new height of awareness where only peace and love prevail. Never again to taste the bitterness of sin. The man on the hill stands in the open door and beckons all to enter therein.

THE SPOKEN WORD

Through the power of the word, God created this universe and all there is in it, along with all of the wonders of heaven. Like the rolling out of a scroll heaven and earth was put in their place, there to stay until the end of time. The heavens reveal the beauty of God's creation; the earth reveals His Majesty and His love for mankind. The mysteries therein are many, and have been challenged and argued over ever since God created man and put him on the face of the earth. The Bible is very clear as to how God created heaven and earth, the explanation is also clear, God has the power to create whatever He chooses through the spoken word. In lack of faith, man has and will continue to argue the pros and cons of creation. Science takes the view that everything has a scientific explanation as to its origin and cannot seem to grasp that there is a higher power capable of doing whatever it chooses to do. Those of faith accept through faith that there is a God and that He and He alone created heaven and earth through His Son, Jesus Christ.

The concept that a spiritual being can create tangible objects through the spoken word has mystified those who proclaim that a tangible object cannot be created out of nothing. If this were not so then it would not be found in Holy Scripture, for God has no untruth in Him and incapable of lying. On the other hand, Satan and his fallen angels reside here on earth and no truth is found in them. Satan is a liar and the father of all lies and will try to distort the truths about God and lead people astray. It is a spiritual battle that we fight here on earth between good and evil. Those who reject the Bible's explanation of creation have been duped by Satan, fallen prey to his deceptive ways.

Satan is an evil force in this world and has the power of deception and doubt. These are his main tools in his effort to cloud the minds of man to the truths of God. The only power Satan has over anyone is the power that they themselves give him, for Satan only has the power of deception and doubt and cannot force anyone to do something against their will. Satan will continue to exist here on earth until the second coming of Jesus Christ and then Christ will cast Him and his fallen angels into the bottomless pit for one thousand years and eventually be thrown into the lake of fire along with all other un-believers, there they will be tormented forever and ever.

Jesus gave all permission to use His name in their battle against Satan and his deceptive ways. By exercising that permission, we can thwart the temptations of Satan through the spoken word. The spoken word being Jesus Christ, the Son of God, our Lord and our Savior. The power of the spoken word will bring all things to pass.

THE TREE
OF CALVARY

O blessed tree of Calvary, blessed was thee when Jesus gave His
life you and me.

He carried with Him our sins to bear, He bore them and paid the
price of sin and set us free.

With His sacrifice He opened the door to our heavenly Father and
became the pathway to eternity.

The angels ministered unto Him as he hung upon that tree and gave
His all so that we could be free.

He regretted not the sacrifice He made, for He knew that He was
fulfilling His Father's will.

He served His time among us sinners and picked twelve to continue
His ways.

Served Him well they did, they spread His word to all who would hear,
we of today are called to do the same.

The tree of Calvary is but a symbol of that time of old when our Lord
and Savior gave His all for those who seek to do his will.

It will stand forever as a monument to the Son of God, the only one
Who can set us free from the sins that now bind us.

Christ gave His life upon the tree of Calvary for you and for me, be
ever grateful by submitting to His will.

THREE OLD NAILS

The centurion went in search of some nails large enough to hold Jesus to the cross at Calvary.

He searched the town o'er and o'er, he finally found three old nails that he thought for sure could hold Jesus to the tree.

He picked them up, light they seemed, so back to Calvary he trod.

On the way the three old nails began to burden his soul, but on he trod and proceeded to nail Jesus to the tree.

Just before the ninth hour of the day the skies grew dark, the lighting flashed while the thunder roared, the graves of the Saints were opened, they rose from the dead and praised God's holy name.

As Jesus hung upon that tree the veil in the temple ripped in two, from the top to the bottom it tore, exposing the holy of holies to all, not just a few.

The centurion was convicted of what he had done. He turned to Jesus and confessed his sin of buying those three old nails and nailing him to that tree at Calvary.

The centurion was freed from his sin of nailing Jesus to that tree.

Even though those three old nails held Jesus to that tree at Calvary it was your sin and my sin that really held Jesus to that tree.

You see, no old nails, no matter how big could hold Jesus to that tree unless he was willing to give his life for you and me.

TICK-TOCK

Life is but a fleeting moment in the passage of time.

It neither stops or waits for anyone, it is a tick and
a tock of the clock that will never stop until
the end of time.

Life is but a shadow of a cloud that is here for the
moment until the wind of time blows it
on its way.

We are no more born until it is time to die, life is no
more than a fleeting moment in the passage
of time.

The interlude between birth and death is full of
sorrows and pain, mixed with some
pleasures it never stays
the same.

When we are young we cannot wait until we grow
old, by the time we realize that we have grown
old it is time to pass on.

The tick and tock that I heard when I was young
came from the clock of life that started
when I was born.

The tick and tock that I now hear is from the clock
of life that is about to run down.

Whether I live or die the tick tock of life's clock will
never stop until the end of time.

A strange analogy it may be, to compare the tick
tock of a clock to life, but I believe that this
is the way that life passes, one tick,
one tock at a time.

Once started life's clock never stops, we just pass
on to a new dimension where there is no
tick or tock, not even the passage
of time.

TIME, FRIEND OR FOE

Time can be likened to a spring fed stream, it neither stops nor does it slow down. Once the water passes where you are standing it is gone and will never return, instead it just keeps going. As it has been aptly said, "Time nor a flowing stream waits for no man."

For the most of us it is only when we reach old age do we realize just how fast time does pass. Therefore, while we are young we should seek the Lord and live by His laws. In the Scriptures, we find that it is to our advantage to seek the Lord first and He in turn will supply our every need. Need being what we need to sustain ourselves, such as a job, by which we can earn a living.

God has ordained from the beginning that this existence has a limited amount of time and after that eternity. Eternity has no time, just the ever present now. Those who accept God's Son, Jesus Christ, as their Lord and Savior and have come to Him for forgiveness of their sins will spend eternity in His presence; all others will be cast from God's sight in what we refer to as hell. How we live our lives here on earth determines where we will spend eternity.

Time is the means by which man measures how long something or somebody has existed. In the state in which we now live it is difficult to perceive the statement, "There shall be no more time." In our present existence, we would be lost without time; we judge things and events by time, work, play, rest, sleep, vacations, devotion to God and a host of other things. Time is not ours to waste, but many do by indulging in sinful acts that distract them from spiritual obligations. One of Satan's ploys is to try to make us believe that we have all of the time in the world to do as we want to please the flesh and that we will have eternity to seek God. This is a lie; for once, we step through the door of death, it is too late to change or seek God. We cannot go back and change anything.

Time is both our friend and our enemy, our friend in the respect that while we are young we have time to change and to seek God, but once we become old we are already set in our ways and find it hard to make changes. This is when time works against us. Often we use the excuse that we will change tomorrow, mostly because we do not want to give up whatever it is that is giving us pleasure for the moment. The truth is that we may not have tomorrow to change, for no man knows when it is his or her time to leave this world, only God knows that.

Therefore, we cannot listen to Satan if we intend to spend eternity in the presence of God. There are those who proclaim that we all will end up in the same place after death so why should we change now? All shall stand before God, He in turn will assign us where we will spend eternity, and we will have no say in where that will be, heaven or hell. We can however assure ourselves where we will send eternity by accepting Jesus Christ as our

Lord and Savior now and comply with His ways of living. Take time to seek God now while He can still be found. Do not be one of those who leave things to the last minute, there may not be a last minute. Death seals where we will spend eternity. Do not waste whatever time you may have left by fulfilling the lusts of the flesh, use time to your advantage and assure yourself where you will spend eternity, the results will be well worth the effort.

TRIALS OF BEING A CHRISTIAN

Christians have been persecuted and looked down on ever since the days of Adam and Eve. Those who deny God have persecuted them. In their way of thinking to believe in God would interfere in the way that they live. They want to live their lives their way and not have to account to anyone as to how they conduct their lives. They also find it difficult to believe in someone whom they can neither see nor touch.

Early Christians were persecuted beyond belief, fed to the wild beasts as their captors watched and cheered, thousands were nailed to a cross to die a prolonged torturous death, and others were stoned to death. They preferred death rather than to deny God. All of Jesus' disciples chose the same death, for to die for Christ is gain.

It was not an easy choice to become a Christian, doing so they knew that they were putting their lives in jeopardy and yet they preferred death rather than a life of servitude to pagan gods. God offered them freedom from oppression and life beyond the grave. To them it was better to die a Christian than to live as a slave. Their courage has given us of today the inspiration and fortitude to stand in face of adversity and proclaim the word of God to the pagans of today.

Today in what we call, modern times Christians are still being persecuted for their belief in God and in some cultures are being put to death for their belief in God and what He represents. The years have changed but the persecution has not. It is a spiritual battle that has been going on ever since Adam and Eve first sinned in the Garden of Eden and it will continue until the second coming of Jesus Christ.

God has given each of us the choice of how we want to conduct our lives and whom we want to serve, God or Satan. To follow God gives us the courage to live a life pleasing to Him and to face life's adversities with the confidence that through God we can overcome the difficult times of life. God does not promise a life free from the adversities of life but he does promise that He will walk with us through our adversities and give us the strength and knowledge to overcome them. My Grandfather once told me, "Man can take away everything that you have and even your life, but man cannot touch your spirit or what you believe."

The battle between good and evil has been going on ever since the beginning of time and basically has not changed in how it is conducted. In each generation God raises up different people who stand in the face of adversity and proclaim His word to all who will listen and many there are who have paid the ultimate price. The more the ungodly tries to extinguish the word of God the more it spreads and it will continue to spread until it is heard in every nook and cranny of the world. All who perpetrate evil will one day succumb to the evil that they profess and suffer the rigors of hell for their rejection of God.

It is here in this world that we as Christians must settle our differences, whether it is between nations or individuals. This is where the battle between good and evil is won or lost. Those who deny God and his sovereignty face eternity separated from God in a place more commonly known as Hell, those who subscribe to the teachings of Jesus Christ (the Son of God) shall inherit the kingdom of God and live in His presence for eternity.

TRUST AND OBEY

Have the problems of the world and personal loss got you down, has the loss of a job or death of a family member got you wondering if there is any justice in this world, has your personal problems and health got you down and you cannot see where your next paycheck is going to come from?

This old world is a tough place to live in at times, you pray and pray and yet things don't seem to change, when will it all end and how will it end bounces around in your mind, and things still don't change.

At one time or another we all face problems in life that seem to get worse as time goes by, we get so involved in our own problems that we forget who is in control, in fact God knows all and is in control of all of our circumstances.

God will and does allow us to go through troubling times, times when we cannot see the forest for the trees because of our own problems, this is when we need to stop and take account of our relationship with God and go to Him in prayer and unload our problems on Him.

Then step back and give God time to bring us answers to our problems, these answers may not be as we would like them to be and yet they are exactly what we need at the time, question not the wisdom of God for He may just be trying to teach us a lesson, a lesson that will allow us to grow in our relationship with Him.

It is harder to do than it is to say, the more our problems press in on us the more we are to pray and cling to the fact that God really is in control and for those who love Him and trust Him will in the end find answers to their problems, God directed answers.

It is through trust and love for God that we are able to control our urges to rebel against God and throw our hands up in defeat, Satan wants us to go down in defeat and will prod us to turn against God and at times his urging can be overwhelming and supposedly the easy way out, when in fact it is just the opposite of what God wants us to do.

Trying times are times when our faith in God is put to the test, it is not easy to do but we must reverse our thinking and hold fast to what we know to be true in the light of God's word, for God will neither forsake us nor leave us alone to face our earthly problems by ourselves, when we think that He is not there is just the time that He comes closest to us.

In the trying times of today it is easy to become anxious about the future and what God has in store for us, but just as God provides for the birds of the air and the creatures of the forest so will He provide for His children, thus it behooves us to exercise our trust in God and allow His love to quiet our anxieties, as it has been expressed many times in the scriptures; "Trust and Obey.".

WE CONTROL OUR
OWN DESTINY

When Jesus ascended into heaven, He sat at the right hand of God and he will sit in the judgment seat of the great Day of Judgment. In this capacity, He will pass judgment on all as they pass before Him and His judgment will be just, according to how they lived their lives here on earth. To those who lived a righteous life will inherit eternal life, all others will be cast from God's sight forever and spend eternity in the lake of fire.

As someone once put it, "It would be better to reign in hell, than to serve in heaven." With such an attitude this person will surly end up in hell. The only difference being that he will not reign in hell, for in hell no one will have contact with anyone; they will suffer all by themselves and call out in anguish for relief from the torment.

The die is cast right here on earth, this is where we have the chance to change and avoid the rigors of hell. While living on earth we live as best suits us and God will honor whichever way we choose to live. God has set commandments by which He wants us to live and if we live in accordance to these commandments, we will inherit eternal life, but if we deny Jesus Christ He in turn will deny us before the throne of God and will have condemned ourselves to hell. God would that no one chooses that type of life, but He has left it to each one as to how they want to conduct themselves while here on earth. Living a righteous life will not automatically allow us to inherit eternal life; we must first accept Jesus Christ as the Son of God and then go on to live a righteous life.

The laws that man makes to govern his life is like the grass of the field, they bend with whichever way the winds blow and man changes them to suit himself. On the other hand, God's laws do not bend with the wind, they are if you will set in concrete for all time and are as they were when He first revealed them. God never changes, man changes from generation to generation and when man chooses to change or disregard the laws of God, he is in fact condemning himself to hell. There is great rejoicing in heaven when one of us sinners makes the decision to live according to the laws of God.

Some of us have to be torn down to our foundation before we come to the realization that only through Jesus Christ can we be saved. This is when we are the most venerable to the temptations of Satan, looking for an easy way out; this is also the time we can take our first steps in our pursuit of living a more Christ-like way of life. Holding Jesus' hand and looking to Him for guidance will lead us back to the road of righteousness and embolden us to turn our lives over to Jesus and walk the pathway of the righteous.

God has promised all who accept His Son, Jesus Christ, as the guardian of his or her life will in no way be turned away, but those who choose to live life their way and by their own rules will face the judgment. This whole way of life comes down to, "Who do you want to follow, Jesus Christ or Satan?" Jesus Christ leads to eternal life, Satan leads to hell. One's destiny is in their own hands and there's alone.

WHEN MY JOURNEY IS OVER

Soon my blood will no longer surge through my veins and the sweet air will no longer grace my lungs.

My lips will become dry and no longer kiss the hand of my bride or kiss the cheeks of my offspring.

My eyes will not perceive the beauty that surrounds my still body, for in death they are closed.

My legs will no longer propel my body down the road of life or walk the seashore of old.

My ears will no longer hear the call of the wild or listen to mockingbirds call.

My taste buds will no longer become excited by the exotic food of the wild.

I will no longer feel your touch as I once did when we embraced under the full of the moon.

My bones will be bleached by the midday sun and the thrills of this life will have faded from view.

Not all will be lost; my soul will have left this frail body with my last breath.

It will soar into the heavens high overhead and return from whence it came.

It will be embraced by the love of our heavenly Father and stand in judgment of my earthly deeds.

My eyes will be opened to a new world that I was unable to see before and no longer will I be led astray by sin.

My ears will hear the strains of heavenly music and I will drink of the waters of eternal life.

I will taste of the fruit of the tree of life and hunger no more for my earthly home.

I will dwell in the house of the Lord, a house not made by hands, but by the word of God.

The fear of darkness (sin) will no longer be, the "Light" of God will guide me on the paths of righteousness and I will sing praises unto Hs Holy name.

My new body will no longer be subject to the whims of man, it will no longer be frail and feel the pain of sin or disease.

It will be free from all earthly ties and I will dwell in the house of the Lord forever. The door of life is open to all who seek it.

When my earthly life is over, I will return to my heavenly home where only love prevails. I follow my ancestors and soon so must you.

Fear not death, for all who accepts Jesus Christ as the Son of God shall live forever.

For those I leave behind I say, "Seek the Lord while you still have the breath of life and the time."

WHICH CROSS HAVE YOU CHOSEN

When Jesus was crucified on the cross at Calvary there were two thieves crucified with Him, one on His left and one on His right.

Jesus' cross has come to be known as the cross of Salvation, the cross on His left represents the cross of redemption, while the cross on His right represents the cross of condemnation.

The thief on the cross of condemnation rejected Jesus as just another criminal deserving of death and also rejected Jesus as being the one who could cleanse him of his sins, thus he died never accepting Jesus as His Lord and Savior, and he died a death in which he would be separated from his creator for eternity.

The thief on the cross of redemption rebuked the other thief claiming that Jesus was a just man, not deserving of death, for he had done no wrong, he asked Jesus to remember him when he entered his kingdom, Jesus in return assured the second thief that he would be with Him that very day in paradise.

Throughout history man has had and still has the choice of which cross he wants to bear, the cross of redemption or the cross of condemnation, the cross of redemption leads to the cross of salvation, whereas the cross of condemnation leads to the separation from God, Jesus Christ, and the Holy Spirit for eternity.

All who come to Jesus Christ and accept Him as the one and only Son of God, their Lord and Savior will indeed be free from the bondage of sin and will be with Jesus forever, for they have chosen the cross of redemption.

All who live life their way and reject Jesus Christ as being the Son of God and the only means by which they can be saved and enter into the kingdom of God are dead already, they too will share the cross of condemnation as did the thief who rejected Jesus on the cross at Calvary,

Those who reject Jesus Christ will indeed be condemned and spend eternity regretting their decision to reject Jesus Christ as their Lord and Savior, for once death occurs it is too late to change ones mind.

We of today have the same choice to make, follow Jesus Christ or reject Him, by doing nothing has the same results as rejecting Jesus Christ as our Lord and Savior, rejection carries the sentence of eternal death, tormented in the fires of hell forever and ever.

On the other hand those who accept Jesus Christ as the one and only Son of God and claim Him as their Lord and Savior shall indeed enjoy spending eternity with Jesus Christ and be blessed as long as they live here on earth.

It is my choice and your choice as to which cross we pick up and carry to our dying days, we and we alone make our own choice, others can influence us, but cannot make that final choice for us.

It is a monumental decision and cannot be taken lightly, the easy way is to do nothing and go with the flow, this is the same as picking up the cross of condemnation and condemning ones self to hell, while those who choose to follow Jesus die to self and live a self disciplined life and put Jesus Christ first in their lives.

The cross of redemption is not an easy cross to bear, nor was it meant to be, for it test us every step of the way to be sure that this is the cross that we want to bear, the rewards are great and for the most part beyond our comprehension, but one thing we do know and that is that Jesus will walk with us all of the way and when we fall short He will carry us till we see our way clear again.

WHOSES LAWS DO YOU LIVE BY

When it comes to the word of God, there are none so blind as those who do not want to see and none so deaf as those who do not want to hear. They read the Scriptures and say they are just a series of stories put together and they do not see how they apply to them or sit in church on Sunday morning and do not hear a word that the preacher is saying that can benefit them.

The stories of the Bible may be old, but they have stood the test of time and have been a benefit to those who not only see the truths in them, but also hear what they have to say to them. Those who apply the truths of the Bible to their lives grow spiritually and are better equipped to find solutions to life's problems than those who are blind to those same truths. Hearing the truth and ignoring what it is saying tantamount being deaf and living life our way and facing rejection by God on the Day of Judgment. These people are like ducks and let God's word run off their backs like water instead of being like a sponge and absorb God's word into their hearts, to be recalled when needed.

Through Moses God gave us ten simple laws to live life by known as the Ten Commandments, but for the most part we have ignored God's Commandments and have filled books upon books full of manmade laws and we still cannot control the behavior of those whom these laws are intended to control. If we cannot obey God's Commandments how do we expect people to live by manmade laws? God's Commandments never change whereas we change our laws to fit different situations as they arise. This shows the arrogance of man, trying to control the behavior of others and not necessarily their own behavior.

Following the Ten Commandments frees us from the burden of manmade laws; the Ten Commandments supersede manmade laws, they cover every part of our behavior and how we should live. Those who live by the Ten Commandments enjoy life much more than those who struggle with manmade laws and what laws of man that they may or may not have broken. Just as the Hebrew people while in the desert turned from the Ten Commandments and worshiped idols so do we of today, we think these Commandments to be archaic and outdated for what we call modern living, when in fact God's Ten Commandments are the only laws that anyone will ever need to control their behavior.

Listen closely to what the Bible has to say and you can hear the voices of the past saying, "Repent, listen to God's word and apply it to your life. Seek God while there is still time, for you know not the day of your demise." Take this advice and return to the Master's flock where the ravaging wolves of this world cannot devour you and you lose your way and be lost forever in the sins of this world. Pray that God will give you insight to see beyond this existence and see the joy and peace that awaits those who live according to His word.

This life is a time of trials and tribulations, a time to grow in the sight of God or succumb to the temptations of Satan and become blind to the truths as revealed in the Holy Scriptures. Upon death, there are two doors through which all will pass; one is the door to eternal life and the other is the door to hell. Those who accept Jesus Christ as their Lord and Savior and live life according to the Ten Commandments will have no fear of death or where they will spend eternity. Whereas those who walked the road of life both blind and deaf to the word of God will be cast from God's sight and suffer the anguish and torture of hell. Everyone can live life according to his or her desire and each one will be held responsible for his or her choice and be assigned his or her place in eternity accordingly.